MW01634046

Old Earth?
Why Not!

James I. Nienhuis

Genesis Veracity
Houston, Texas

2003

www.GenesisVeracity.com

Genesis Veracity
P.O. Box 850
5773 Woodway Drive
Houston, Texas 77057
1-866-GEOFACT

ISBN Number: 0-9726206-0-5
Library of Congress Number: 2002095802

Library of Congress Cataloguing in Publication Data

Nienhuis, James I. — 1954
Old Earth? Why Not! / by James I.
Nienhuis. — 1st ed. p. cm.
Includes Bibliographical References

1. Geology 2. Natural Selection 3. Ice Age
4. Astronomy 5. Human Evolution
6. Biblical History 7. Archaeology

The Book Connection Consultants
Editor — M.A.S. Stautberg
Cover Design — Gladys Ramirez
Book Design & Layout — Rita Mills

The paper used in this publication meets the requirements of the American National Standard for Permanence of Paper for Printed Library Materials Z39.48-1984.

Printed in the United States of America

Table of Contents

(Claims That Shall Be Refuted)

Old Earth?
Why Not!

Foreword

We have been taught theories of an old earth and Darwinian evolution that have little scientific basis and defy Biblical history. What is observed in nature and anthropology, and what the Bible says about earth history, actually contradict prevailing scientific thought. In this book, I will mention some of the claims made by mainstream scientists, and rebut them, chapter by chapter. Please attempt to neutralize any prejudice, and look at the facts.

CLAIM 1

Dinosaurs Died Out About 65 Million Years Ago

If you accept this premise, there should be no known human contact with dinosaurs in history. You judge if there has been recent interaction between humans and "dinosaurs."

The word "dinosaur" was not used until 1841, when a British scientist, Sir Richard Owen, while studying the fossils of large reptiles, decided they were a new order of animal, and named them dinosaurs (which means terrible lizards). Throughout history, these "terrible lizards" have encountered humans, and many of the encounters took place in Sir Owens' own British Isles.

From *The History of the British Kings,* translated from a now unknown ancient Welsh language by Geoffry of Monmouth, we learn that King Morvidus (who ruled around 330 B.C.) was devoured by a large reptilian monster. The account states that the creature "gulped down the body of Morvidus as a big fish swallows a little one." The animal was called a belua.[1]

A monster at Buries in Suffolk, England is reported in a chronicle from 1405 A.D.:

> "Close to the town of Buries, near Sudbury, there has lately appeared, to the great hurt of the countryside, a dragon, vast in body, with a crested head, teeth like a saw, and a tail extending to an enormous length. Having slaughtered the shepherd of a flock, it devoured many sheep." After failed attempts by local archers to kill the beast, due to its tough hide: . . . "in order to destroy him, all the country people around were summoned. When the dragon saw that he was again to be assailed by arrows, he fled into a marsh or mere and there hid himself among the long reeds, and was no more seen."[2]

British government officials apparently were unaware that flying reptiles had been extinct for millions of years when they reported in 1793 A.D.:

> "In the end of November and beginning of December last, many of the country people observed...dragons, appearing in the north and flying rapidly towards the east, from which they concluded, and their conjectures were right, that . . . boisterous weather would follow."[3]

The lore and literature of Great Britain are peppered with other accounts of reptilian giants. Hundreds of sightings of the "Loch Ness Monster" have made news; but over forty sightings on Loch Morar, and other sightings on Lochs Lomond, Awe, and Rannoch have not made the news.[4] Over 100 townships of Britain have reported dragons throughout their histories; yet, they went extinct 65 million years ago?

Apollonius of Tyana, traveler and historian from 2,000 years ago, noted that ". . . the whole of India is girt with enormous dragons, in marshes and mountains."[5] He said that the marsh dragons were 30 cubits (about 60 feet) long, sluggish, with black skin, and fewer scales than the mountain dragons. Apollonius chronicled these mountain dragons as being golden in color, of great length, fast as a river, and killers of elephants.[6]

The Roman historian, Pliny the Elder, said that in India the elephants are constantly at war with the dragons. He noted that the dragons would leap from trees onto passing elephants, bite their trunks and eyes, and coil about them. The elephants tried to scrape the dragons off on the trees, but the dragons' coiling constriction and venom killed the elephants, which then fell dead upon the dragons and fatally crushed them. Likewise, the dragons would hide in waterholes and ambush the elephants, with the same ensuing struggles and results.[7]

Marco Polo, upon his return from Asia, reported of families raising dragons, yoking them to royal chariots for special occasions, and using dragon parts for medicinal purposes.[8] Interestingly, the twelve signs of the Chinese zodiac are animals, eleven of which are everyday, extant creatures (rat, horse, dog, ox, rabbit, tiger, snake, ram, monkey, rooster, dog, and pig.) The twelfth is the dragon. Why would the Chinese include the "mythological" dragon with these common living animals?

Herodotus, a Greek historian from around 400 B.C., wrote that serpents soared in the skies of Arabia.[9] (This winged serpent, called by the natives "Kongamato," apparently still flies in southern Africa.[10])

The Sioux Indians of America tell of a 20-foot

wingspan flying creature being hit by lightning, and made pictures of this creature; this may be is the infamous "Thunderbird" which has been in American Indian lore for centuries.[11]

Two Arizona cowboys, as reported in the "Tombstone Epitaph" newspaper, killed a large flying reptile in 1890.[12] The creature reportedly had an eight foot alligator-like head with a mouth full of teeth. The cowboys cut of its wing tip (which was a tough membrane, like a bat's) for a trophy.

Nerluc, France was renamed in honor of a dragon killing. The animal reportedly was larger than an ox with long, sharp horns.[13]

The well-known old European science book, "Historia Animalium," says that dragons were not extinct in the 1500's A.D., but were very rare and relatively small.[14]

In the Bible, the book of Job 40:15 (probably from about 2000 B.C.) describes in great detail the Behemoth. Huge, lumbering and living in swamps, it had a tail "like a cedar tree." Evolutionists claim this creature was an elephant or hippopotamus; but with a tail like a cedar tree? I think not.

The Anasazi Indans of the American southwest made pictures on rocks showing dinosaurs and men.[15] A thick coat of "desert varnish" on these images proves that these pictures were created many hundreds of years ago. Desert varnish (windblown pollen and dust) slowly accumulates on rocks in the desert; the varnish on the Anasazi pictures is so thick that they must have been drawn many hundreds of years ago.[16] Therefore, these art works are not frauds perpetrated by mischievous European newcomers (who had no motive for such a fraud), but were made by natives long ago, showing men and dragons living together.

In South America, burial stones from the Ica Stones reveal creatures that look like triceratops, pterosaurs, and tyrannosaurus rexes coexisting with humans.[17]

On Dec.11, 1999 villagers near Boboa, New Guinea saw a huge swimming lizard, as reported in "The Independent" newspaper of Papua, New Guinea. The newspaper also declared that the following day, a pastor and church elder saw the animal not far from the first sighting. The creature was described as having a body "as long as a dump truck and nearly two meters wide, with a long neck and long slender tail." It was walking on hind legs as thick "as thick as a coconut palms' tree trunk," and had two smaller forelegs. The head was similar in shape to a cow's, with large eyes and "sharp teeth as long as fingers." The skin was like a crocodile, and it had "largish scoops on its back."[18]

The Roman historian, Dio (also known as Cassius),

wrote that one day, when Regulus, a Roman consul (third century B.C.), was fighting against Carthage (North Africa), a dragon suddenly crept up and settled behind the wall of the Roman army. The Romans killed it by order of Regulus, skinned it, and sent the hide to the Roman Senate. When the dragon was measured by order of the Senate, it turned to be an amazing 120 feet long, and the thickness was fitting to the length.[19]

Were the thousands of people who have seen gigantic reptiles all hallucinating? This is highly unlikely. The evidence is overwhelming that dinosaurs did not go extinct 65 million years ago. To ignore the plethora of dinosaur sightings and detailed descriptions is akin to the proverbial ostrich with its head in the sand.

CLAIM 2

Dinosaur Fossils Are Millions Of Years Old

Since dinosaurs have been with us throughout history, one wonders if the dinosaur fossils are as old as advertised (65-150 million years old). Fossils formed when sand and clay covered dead or dying organisms at the bottom of a body of water. Subsequently, the water receded from these sedimentary deposits, allowing them to dry out and harden into rock, and thus, encased the organisms.

If these creatures did die and fossilize millions of years ago, no organic material should be present in the fossils, as this material would have disintegrated or been mineralized, millions of years ago. But lo and behold, fossils have been discovered containing residual organic material, thus indicating the fossils are in the thousands, not millions, of years of age. This should not surprise us, as dinosaurs are inextricably linked to human history.

Organic osteocalcyn was found in dinosaurs' bones, as reported by Gerhard Muyzer.[1] This bone protein should have long ago randomly decomposed, or turned into rock (mineralized) by mineral-rich waters percolating through the entombed creature and its surrounding rock, presuming the bones are millions of years old.

In Mongolia, a mother dinosaur fossil was excavated which was brooding upon 22 eggs.[2] The presence of protein in buried dinosaur eggs is highly surprising considering the chemical instability of protein.[3]

Faculty and staff at Montana State University were shocked to discover that a tyrannosaurus rex bone contained red blood cells. These old earth, evolutionist researchers ran six different tests, attempting to prove they were not red blood cells.[4] But all the tests came back positive, causing panic for mainstream earth scientists; though predictably, the test results were not front-page news, as the other revelations of allegedly anomalous organic presence were not.

Dinosaur bones have been discovered in Alberta, Canada that are encased within ironstone nodules.

"The nodules prevented water from invading the bones which, for all intents and purposes, cannot be distinguished from modern bones."[5]

Bones have been found in northern Alaska for decades which until recently were assumed to be of buffalos because they are so fresh looking and un-fossilized. When scientists arrived and analyzed the bones, they determined the bones were of duck-billed dinosaurs.[6] Fresh, unmineralized dinosaur bones totally defy the notion that they are millions of years old.

Most dinosaur bones discovered contained the original bone[7] that should have randomly decomposed over the hypothesized millions of years of their burial within the sedimentary strata. The presence of organic material in the specimen described in this chapter defies the hypothesis of dinosaur extinctions 65 millions years ago, as do the hundreds of "dragon" encounters with humans noted in the previous chapter. These contradictions shall be resolved as we look further into the available evidence.

CLAIM 3

Sedimentary Rocks Were Formed Gradually, Over Millions Of Years

"Old earthers" (a generic term that we will use to designate those who embrace the hypothesis that the earth is billions of years old) would have us believe that the ancient ocean rose and receded many times over millions of years, leaving sediments on the continents with each recession. With each new encroachment of the ocean onto the continents, more sediment was deposited on top of the previously deposited sediments which, by then, presumably were rock-hard (as they would have been on dry land for millions of years until the next encroachment of the ocean). Allegedly, these sediments gradually covered up the organisms that had sunk to the bottom. Then, when the water receded, the sediments solidified around the organisms to form fossils.

One of the problems with this theory is that sedimentary layers in the geologic column cover states, countries, and occasionally entire continents; and when they don't cover entire continents, they grade into other sedimentary rock types, proving these layers were deposited on the bottom of a body of water which completely covered the continents.[1] (The mountains uplifted later, as explained in Chapter 4.)

If the sedimentary rocks truly did result from many encroachments and recessions of the ocean, on and off the continents, the deposits laid down would only cover the area of river deltas, say 50 miles by 50 miles (which is a good average for the areal extent of deltas). This is because most of the sediments accumulating today are at the mouths of rivers. These sediment accumulation areas are the river deltas.

In the old earther's scenario, when the ocean encroached, the rivers still dumped sediment into the risen ocean, only farther inland. Then, when the sea level fell again, a deposit of sediment the size of a delta would be left on the land. This deposit would then solidify into rock. However, since the deposits we see in the geologic column cover much larger areas (states, countries, continents), the scenario of the sea level rising and falling is implausible. Apparently, the expansive sedimentary strata were laid down at the bottom of a body of water that completely covered the continents, that is a global flood.

One phenomenon of the sedimentary rock layers that suggests rapid sedimentation is polystratic trees. (Polystratic means "of many strata.") These trees were fossilized in a vertical position within the rock column, transecting multiple layers of sedimentary strata.[2] So, according to the old earthers, these trees stayed upright for millions of years, planted in the bottom of a body of water, while sediments slowly built up around them. However, trees flooded by newly dammed rivers will rot and fall over, certainly within hundreds of years. So, we are supposed to believe that these fossilized trees, in a vertical position, stayed planted and vertical for millions of years while sediments slowly built up around them? Such a scenario is difficult to rationalize.

These polystratic trees are usually no more than 20 feet tall, having been broken off at the roots and top. These trees were uprooted and transported by a devastating flood, and were deposited in a vertical position, due to the weight of the root balls. Once the uprooted trees were deposited in this vertical mode, sediments rapidly built up around them, before there was time for the trees to rot, degrade, and fall over. Rapid, catastrophic flooding and sedimentation provided the water energy and sediment-load to inundate and bury these trees.

Another problem with the gradual sedimentation over millions of years scenario, is that in order for the ocean to come up on the land, either the continental earth crust must drop, or the oceanic crust must rise. The continental and oceanic earth crusts sit atop the earth's mantle. The mantle is a highly pressurized, semi-molten magma (lava within the earth) zone between the earth's crust and the earth's core.

Continental crust is less dense than oceanic crust, and so rides higher atop the mantle than does the oceanic crust; and thus, for the continents to drop, the minerals that compose continental crust must spontaneously become denser, relative to oceanic crust. And for oceanic crust to rise, it must also defy geochemistry by having its minerals mysteriously become less dense, and so float higher on the mantle, relative to the continental crust. Predictably, there is no physical geological evidence of such transformations.

Old earthers want us to believe that animals died and were slowly covered up over many years by sediments slowly settling out at the bottom of a body of water. Then the water receded, leaving the sediments and organisms to begin to dry and harden into rock.

There is a problem, however: when an animal dies in water, scavengers attack, bacteria attack, and within a matter of weeks, there are few, if any, signs of the animal. Yet according to the old earthers, the dead organisms were covered during hundreds of years, and remained at the bottom for millions of years, until the next ocean recession occurred. This is impossible because the organisms would have totally disarticulated and been devoured within only months.

Obviously, sediments rapidly entombed these organisms, and shortly thereafter, the water drained away, allowing the sediments to quickly harden, before there was time for the organisms to rot and be scavenged away. The mechanics of the Great Flood provide the means for this rapid fossil formation, and shall be explained in Chapter 9.

Billions of clams were entombed in the sedimentary layers on the continents. Strangely, often the fossilized clams' two shells are closed. When clams die, within a couple of hours their shells open up. Therefore, sediments must have rapidly entombed these clams, before they had time to open up.[3] It is impossible that these dead clams were covered over up slowly, over many years.

Massive fossil graveyards can be seen in sedimentary rocks in various parts of the world.[4] The animals therein were mangled and piled together in a catastrophic sedimentary event. The sediments and entombed organisms then quickly dried and hardened, as discussed earlier. Many different kinds of animals and plants from various ecological environments are amassed in these fossil graveyards, strongly suggesting that a huge flow of water carried these animals and plants, until they were entombed together in sediments.

An 80-foot long fossilized skeleton of a baleen whale was discovered during mining operations in a quarry in Lompoc, California in 1976; the whale was "standing" on its tail in a vertical position within the sedimentary rock layers.[5] The whale fossil transected layers that allegedly accumulated over millions of years. Is it plausible to assume that when the whale died, it balanced on its tail for millions of years on the sea floor while sediments slowly built up around it?

Some 300 tetrapods (two foot-long reptiles) were discovered in "260-million-year-old" clay and sandstone strata in Russia. These tetrapods were buried standing on their tails (in a vertical orientation) with their necks extended upward.[6] The sediments entombing these creatures are said to have accumulated at a rate of millimeters per year; therefore, the creatures must have stood on their tails for thousands of years while the sediments slowly built up around them. No, obviously, they were rapidly entombed to facilitate their verticality.

Here is a startling fact that shoots another hole in the old earth scenario: at current rates of land erosion, the continents would be leveled to sea level within 15 million years.[7] And yet, they say that the fossils and rocks of continental strata are up to 500 million years old. Therefore (inconveniently), their 500- million-year-old rocks should have eroded away about 485 million years ago.

If the ocean has been rising and receding repeatedly over millions years, leaving behind sedimentary layers with each recession, one would expect erosion features (valleys, river channels) to form in the sedimentary layers while the ocean was receded. Then when the ocean rose again, new sediment should have filled in these erosion features. In-filled erosion features are not seen in the geologic strata.[8] Generally seen, however, are layers of rock stacked like pancakes, indicating that they were laid down rapidly and consecutively, in one flood episode.

Remember that these stacks of pancake-like rock layers cover states, countries, and occasionally, entire continents, and when they don't cover entire continents, they grade into other rock types. Organisms were rapidly entombed and lithified in these vast sheets of sediments, before they degraded. Polystratic trees transect horizontal rock layers that allegedly built up over millions of years, and yet, must have built up rapidly. All the evidence suggests one devastating flood event that covered the continents and left behind vast layers of sediments with billions of entombed organisms therein: Noah's Flood!

CLAIM 4

Mountains Uplifted About 65 Million Years Ago

Old earthers believe that the mountain ranges of the world uplifted about 65 million years ago, about the same time that dinosaur extinctions supposedly happened. We have seen that dinosaurs' fossils are in the thousands of years of age (discussed in Chapter 2); therefore, logically, the mountains uplifted only thousands of years ago, shortly after these creatures were entombed in sediments.

Within some mountains of the world are warped sedimentary rock layers containing multitudinous fossils. These layers are warped because of horizontal, regional compression; the sedimentary layers, which had been deposited on the continents, were warped or folded. (This warping and folding was often accompanied by plutonic magma upwelling from the mantle below, which uplifted the mountains further, as discussed in Chapter 9.)

If the mountains uplifted about 65 million years ago (slight residual uplift still occurs, but not residual from nearly that long ago), the sedimentary layers that were folded in that uplift must be older than 65 million years. Most sedimentary rocks are said to be 100 to 500 million years old. Much of the folded sedimentary rocks in the mountains are purportedly in this age range. But, a 300-million-year-old sedimentary deposit would have become solid rock well within the 235 million years (of encroachments and recessions of the sea) which ostensibly led up to the 65 million year mark, at which point, the mountain building is said to have begun.

Since the sedimentary layers should have been solid rock by the time the folding began, when they folded, radial tension cracks should have developed in the warped (folded) rock layers. Take a thin slab of rock and bend it hard, what happens? It cracks. Likewise, the sedimentary rock layers should have cracked when they were folded. However, there are no tension cracks in the folded sedimentary rock layers of the world.[1]

What do we conclude from this absence of tension cracks in the folded sedimentary rocks? Since there are no tension cracks, the sedimentary layers were not hard rock when they were folded. These sedimentary layers were still wet and soft when they were folded, as proven by the absence of radial tension cracks in the folded, now hard, sedimentary layers. All of these layers were wet and soft when the folding occurred. Thus, they were all laid down in one giant flood event, and were folded shortly thereafter, before they solidified into rock.[2] Once again the Flood scenario beautifully explains what is observed in geology.

Remember again, at current rates of land erosion, the continents would be leveled to sea level in under 15 million years. Therefore, any continental rocks, supposedly 15 million years old or older, should have eroded away long ago. (If continents would erode to sea level within 15 million years, all rocks that age and older, which were above sea level on the continents, should have eroded into the sea.) Yet, the vast majority of continental sedimentary rocks are hundreds of millions of years old, as maintained by old earthers. Obviously, the old earth rock date estimates are at least 30 to 40 times too high, in light of the erosion rate (as 30, multiplied by 15 million years equals 450 million years, the supposed age of many sedimentary rocks).

Mountains would be the first land areas to erode down, as they are steep and receive much inclement weather, but they contain rocks supposedly hundreds of millions of years old. Because the mountains would erode down first, then the flatter land areas during the 15-million-year continental erosion down to sea level, the mountains should have vanished within about 1.5 million years.[3]

Yet, rocks are in the mountains that contain simple snails, clams, corals and insect fossils purportedly formed some 500 million years ago when biological evolution was allegedly just beginning. (See Chapter 8 for refutation of evolution over millions of years.) Thus, the old earthers insist that early biological evolutionary history is evident in sedimentary rocks that, in reality, should have eroded away at least 30 times over.

The Greenlander tribes-people know of the global flood, and say that the presence of ocean creature fossils in mountain rocks resulted from that flood (as explained in Chapter 9.) This ancient tribe has a lot more on the ball than most modern scientists. They see that for ocean creatures to be entombed in the sedimentary rocks of mountains, the creatures must have been overwhelmed and entombed by a devastating world inundation; the sedimentary strata is what remained when the floodwater receded into the deepened ocean basins.

And in mountain areas, the folded sedimentary strata have no tension cracks, proving all the sediment of the strata were still wet and soft when they were folded during mountain building at the close of the Flood. The continents thickened (sediment deposition and mountain uplift), as the ocean basins deepened, and the Floodwater slid off into the, then deeper, ocean basins (as explained in Chapter 9).

Volcanoes are another kind of mountain. They result from oceanic plates melting in the mantle, after diving under continental plates, and rising up, as magma, through the continental crust, to exude volcanic material on the earth's surface. Earthquakes are associated with this crust movement.

There are about 50,000 "extinct" volcanoes, and they look little different than active volcanoes. Most of the "extinct" volcanoes supposedly formed about 65 million years ago, when the continental crust collisions were folding sediments in mountains (but with no tension cracks)! However, please recall, all these "65 million year old mountains" should have vanished by erosion well within 15 million years of their formation. Active volcanoes and earthquakes are merely remnants of the massive volcanism of the Flood and early post-Flood years, which resulted from the runaway crustal plate movement.

The oceanic trenches can be thought of as oceanic crustal down-warp, as some continental mountains can be thought of as continental crustal up-warp. Oceanic plates collided and down-warped, to form deep trenches in the ocean bottom (up to six miles deep); similarly, the continental plates collided, and up-warped the sedimentary layers, to help form mountains (as discussed in Chapter 9) up to five miles high.

Loose sediment is gradually accumulating in the oceans, mostly from river mouths. The oceans should have been filled with sediment within 80 million years (as the volume of the oceans is roughly five times the volume of continental rocks that are above sea level, and therefore erosion fated). But the oceanic trenches hold little sedimentary accumulation, which is surprising because the oceanic trenches should have been filled first, as they are at the ocean bottom and sometimes near sediment producing river deltas; so obviously, these trenches are very young because they have little sediment accumulated in them. The trenches formed when the mountains formed, during the runaway crustal plate movement of the Flood (as discussed in Chapter 9).

Through old-earther eyes’, a lot was going on about 65 million years ago, wasn’t there? Dinosaurs were going extinct, mountain ranges were uplifting, thousands of volcanoes were erupting, ocean trenches were down-warping, all at the same time. According to the evidence, however, all these things, except total dinosaur extinction (as noted in Chapter 1), did happen together, but only thousands of years ago, not 65 million.

CLAIM 5

Noah's Flood Is A Fairytale

Hundreds of tribal groups are spread all over the globe. Their oral traditions and legends have been passed down from their ancestors through the generations. One legend is very common among the tribes, like this one from New Guinea:

> "Once a great flood came which covered the whole earth and wiped out everyone on earth except for the ancestors of the Biami people. Those ancestors climbed up into the Gobia Tree, the bark of which they make into string for their string bags. They took up into the tree their planting materials for crops, all their animals, their dogs and their pigs and every-

thing else necessary for life. As the floodwaters rose up on the face of the earth the people climbed further up the tree. They were safe in the branches of this tree because the tree grew up above the waters as the waters rose up. When the waters went down from the surface of the whole earth, the people were able to climb down the tree. The ground was very muddy, but eventually they planted their crops and their animals began to reproduce. They moved away from the tree and began to repopulate the earth. Those who had climbed down out of the tree were the ancestors of the Samos, the Kubos, the Gobasis, and the Etoro."[1]

Over 270 tribes have been documented to be proponents of the notion that the whole world was once inundated by water.[2] Here is one from the Greenlander tribe of Canada:

> "The world once overturned. Some people were turned into fiery spirits, all the rest drowned but one. Afterwards, the survivor smote the ground with his stick, a woman sprung out, and the two of them repopulated the world. Proof of the flood is found in the form of sea fossils on high mountains."[3]

(Fossils of ocean creatures in the mountains will be explained in Chapter 9.)

The details of the basic flood theme vary from tribe to tribe, but obviously, this story was passed down from ancestors who were knowledgeable of the same cataclysmic event, a flood of water unparalleled in human history. The ancient Assyrians knew of this flood:

> "The gods, led by Enlil, agreed to cleanse the earth of an overpopulated humanity, but Utnapishtim was warned by the god Ea in a dream. He and some craftsmen built a large boat (one acre in area, seven decks) in a week. He then loaded it with his family, the craftsmen, and 'the seed of all living creatures'. The waters of the abyss rose up, and it stormed for six days. Even the gods were frightened by the flood's fury. Upon seeing all the people killed, the gods repented and wept. The waters covered everything but the top of the mountain Nisur, where the boat landed. Seven days later, Utnapishtim released a dove, but it returned finding nowhere else to land. He next returned a sparrow, which also returned, and then a raven, which did not return. Thus he knew the waters had receded enough for the people to emerge. Utnapishtim made a sacrifice to the gods."[4]

No other legend pervades the lore of the world's tribes as does the Great Flood. In Africa, the Pygmies (Central Africa), the Kikuyu (Kenya), the Yoruba (southwest Nigeria), the Mandingo (Ivory Coast) and the Kwaya (near Lake Victoria), among others, have ancestral knowledge of the Great Flood.[5]

In North America, the Eskimos and the Innuit (Alaska), the Yakima (Washington state), the Chippewa (Great Lakes), and the Choctaw (southeast U.S.), among others, have generational awareness of a global flood.[6]

In Asia, the Kamchadale (Siberia), the Bahnar (Cochin China) and the Miatso (southern China), the Chingpa (Burma), and the Andaman (Bay of Bengal), among others, know by oral tradition of a cataclysmic flood event.[7]

In Europe; the early Greeks, Germans, Celtics, Vikings, and Welsh, among others, noted the Flood in their lore.[8]

In Central and South America, the Yaqui (northern Mexico), the Nahua (central Mexico), the Maya (Guatemala), the Ipurina (upper Amazon), and the Coroado (southern Brazil), among others, speak of a worldwide deluge in their ancient histories.[9]

In the Pacific Islands and Australia, the Kabadi (New Guinea), the Maori (New Zealand), the Mangaia (Cook Islands), the Gumaidj (northern

Australia), and the Polynesian Hawaiians, among others, know the Big Flood.[10]

In the Middle East, the Zoroastrians (Iran), the Egyptians, the ancient Babylonians (Iraq), the ancient Hittites (Turkey), and the Hebrews (Israel), among others, have recollections of an historical catastrophic deluge.[11]

The Hebrew report in the Bible (Genesis 6,7,8) of this world famous Great Flood is the most well-known account: God was displeased with mankind, so He flooded the earth, killing all that were not on Noah's Ark. The waters flooded the earth for 150 days, then began to recede. The Ark landed in the Mountains of Ararat (Eastern Turkey), then, Noah sent out a raven that did not return. He then sent out a dove that returned with an olive twig. The next week he sent the dove out again it didn't return, so Noah figured it was to time disembark from the Ark.

The Michoacan tribe of Mexico has a similar flood legend:

> "When the floodwaters began to rise, a man named Tezpi entered into a great vessel, taking with him his wife and children and diverse seeds and animals. When the waters abated, the man sent out a vulture, but the bird found plenty of corpses to eat and didn't return. Other birds

> also flew away and didn't return. Finally, he sent out a hummingbird, which returned with a green bough in its beak."[12]

To perceive the Biblical Flood story as fantasy is to call the ancestors of these tribes liars. The politically correct mainstream scientist has a real dilemma here. It seems extremely unlikely that disparate people groups from around the globe, with no interest in copying each other's heritages, would have similar legends of global destruction by water, unless of course, these tribes are actually recounting an historical event. Evidently, there is more to this Flood thing than most people realize.

CLAIM 6

Coal And Oil Deposits Are Millions Of Years Old

Within the Flood-caused sedimentary strata of the continents are vast mats of coal, and pockets of oil and gas. These formed from massive accumulations of organic material (plants and animals) which had been covered by more sediments, and thus compressed, and were subsequently heated.

If the oil and gas pockets are millions of years old, all the gas pressure in the pockets should have been relieved, as the gas would have percolated up through the semi-porous and semi-permeable overlying rock layers. In fact, all of the gas within the strata should have bled up through the overlying rock layers, and escaped into the atmosphere, in less than 100,000 years.[1] And yet, when exploratory drill pipe enters a pocket of oil and gas (which is supposedly hundreds of millions of years old), great gas pressure often releases up the drill hole, a "gusher." The presence of this gas pressure, within the sedimentary strata, tells us that these deposits were formed less than 100,000 years ago.

Imagine an oil and gas field 10,000 feet underground which is said to be 300 million years old. Highly pressurized gas within this deposit would percolate up through the sedimentary rocks (as escaping gas can be monitored on the earth's surface). If this gas percolated up at a rate of only one inch per year, it would escape within 100,000 years; if it percolated up at a rate of .003 inch per year, it would escape to the atmosphere within the alleged 300 million years that the deposit is purported to be. One inch per year is plausible; .003 inch per year is not, as much more viscous matter (water and oil) percolate through rocks at much greater rates than .003 inch per year. (For instance, water tables rapidly rise after long and heavy rainfall.)

The vast mats of coal that we see within the layers of sedimentary strata cover extensive areas, often hundreds of thousands of square miles. The old earthers say that coal was formed in swamps over millions of years as plant debris slowly built up in swamps, and then was covered with new sediment from another ocean encroachment. Ever heard of a swamp, hundreds of miles by hundreds of miles in area, with yards of swamp muck depth? (Like the coal bed that underlies parts of Oklahoma, Missouri, Illinois, Indiana, Kentucky, and Pennsylvania?[2]) These are the dimensions that some of the swamps must have been for the formation of some of the extensive coal beds of the earth, according to the old earth hypothesis.

Old earthers say that coal must have formed over millions of years, because the huge volume of organic material in the deposits requires millions of years worth of plant growth, and then decay, in ancient swamps. However, the volume of organic material in the earth's coal beds represents only 128 years of plant growth, or stated another way, only three times the plant growth as is extant in the world today.[3] So, plant debris accumulations over millions of years would have been millions of times greater than the plant accumulations reflected in coal deposits.

The types of vegetation that compose coal are not often found in swampy environments, but are usually from a mountain-rainforest type environment.[4] Apparently, this vegetation was knocked down and carried by water, until vast mats of vegetation accumulated, and were then rapidly covered by sediments, in a cataclysmic flood event that uprooted trees, eroded the land intensely, then redeposited this material in sedimentary layers that cover the continents.

According to the old earth thesis, most of the coal beds were formed about 250 million years ago. But a young earth geologist took a piece of wood from a coal bed in Australia[5] and sent it to a carbon 14 dating lab, without telling the lab that the wood came from a supposed 250-million-year-old layer. The carbon 14 date calculated it to be about 30 thousand years old. (Even this figure is too high, carbon 14 dating gives inflated ages for reasons to be discussed in Chapter12.) But how can this be? The wood still had enough radioactive carbon 14 in it to show an age in the thousands of years; yet, according to mainstream geologists and evolutionists, the wood was deposited in a swamp from 10,000 times farther back in the past than the residual carbon 14 indicates. Obviously, this coal formed a short time ago in one awesome flood, the Flood of which the tribes of the world are well aware (as discussed in Chapter 5).

Old earthers claim that all the measurements of carbon 14 in coal is due to contamination, but this has been shown to be highly unlikely.[6] The amounts of carbon 14 in most samples are at least five times greater than margins of error pertaining to contamination considerations.

If coal beds really were formed from the vegetation of a swamp, the bottom of the coal beds should show evidence of the roots and soil responsible for the growth of the swamp vegetation. No such evidence is seen. The coal material rests on clean underlying sediment that has no signs of roots or soil.[7] Again, this is further evidence that the vegetative debris must have been transported from another location to the deposition site in a massive flow of water and mud.

Coal layers often contain large tree trunks that were ripped out of the ground from a different location, and transported by a huge flow of water. These tree trunks are ripped at the roots, proving they did not grow where they were deposited.[8] Many of these trunks are the vertical polystratic trees which were discussed in Chapter 3.

Most people think that millions of years are required for vegetative debris to transform into coal. Nothing could be further from the truth. High-grade coal (anthracite) has been manufactured in a lab within a matter of weeks. Vegetative matter was heated and pressurized for a short period of time, and voila, coal.[9] Earth crust dynamics during and after the Flood caused this rapid coalification, and shall be discussed in Chapter 9.

The origin of oil is somewhat a mystery. However, it has been produced in the laboratory in a matter of hours from sewage sludge.[10]

We do know that all the high gas pressure from oil deposits should have percolated up through the semi-porous overlying rock layers and escaped into the atmosphere in under 100,000 years, and that the coal layers of the world contain measurable amounts of carbon 14 that are reflective of their recent deposition; therefore, pressurized oil and gas deposits and extensive coal beds surely formed only thousands of years ago, not millions.

CLAIM 7

Radiogenic Rock Dating Proves That Rocks Are Millions Of Years Old

You may have heard of lava rocks being "potassium-argon dated" or "uranium-lead dated" in the millions of years of age. The old earthers say that these dates of origin for rocks are virtually infallible and scientifically reliable. In reality, these dating methods are extremely unreliable, and are predicated upon several unknowable presuppositions. (The reasons for exaggerated carbon 14 dates for organic remains will be explained in Chapter 12.)

The radiogenic rock dating methodologists measure the amount of radioactive material relative to the amount of stable material in lava rocks. (In the uranium-lead dating method, radioactive uranium decays and becomes stable lead.) The older a rock is, the more radioactive material has decayed and become stable material. So, since the rock daters know the current rates at which radioactive materials decay into stable (non-radioactive) materials, they calculate the amount of time it would take for the original amount of a radioactive material to decay to the current amount of stable material. The time it supposedly took for this decay to occur is the calculated age of the lava rock.

One problem with this scheme is the impossibility of knowing if stable material (like lead) crystallized during the solidification of the rock from lava. If some of the lead formed in this way, radiogenic rock date results would be exaggerated because it would appear that a greater quantity of radioactive uranium had decayed into stable lead than reality would indicate.[1]

The rock daters do know the current rates of radioactive decay, but they do not know that these rates were not different in the past. Once again, they were not there in the distant past to measure decay rates. Decay rates have been altered in the laboratory,[2] so to say that rates have not been different in the past is to deny the possibility that some catastrophic astronomical and/or geophysical event provided an environment for decay rates' variances from today's norms. If the decay rates had been higher, date results would be too old; if the rates were lower, dates for the rocks' formations would be too young.

Lava rocks make up much of the earth's geology. They are found associated with sedimentary rocks in the mountains, and flatter lands, as well. Groundwater is constantly percolating through these various kinds of rocks, from rainwater and subterranean sources. Lightly acidic groundwater removes radioactive material from lava rocks.[3] Rocks dated that had incurred groundwater percolation would show an exaggerated age because much radioactive material had been removed by the lightly acidic groundwater. The rock daters would under-estimate the original quantity of radioactive material in the rock because they couldn't factor in an amount that had been lost to groundwater, and so, inflated rock dates would result.

These three problematic presuppositions of the rock dating methods deal a mortal wound to the believability of these methods. After all, how can the daters know the initial amount of stable material, the constancy of decay rates, and occurrence, or not, of radioactive material removal by lightly acidic groundwater percolation? The dating methods are analogous to someone supposedly knowing how long a burning candle was when it was new, without having measured it when it was new: he knows how fast it is now burning and he knows how much candle remains, so from that, he knows the original length of the candle? Incredible.

Mount St. Helen's blew up in 1980 in the state of Washington. It was a massive volcanic event and the landscape was devastated for miles around. A lava dome rose up during this eruption. Radiogenic rock daters calculated the age of this volcanic extrusion to be about one million years old.[4] And yet, the dome was formed only a few years before it was dated, not one million years before.

In Hawaii, a lava flow known by the natives to be about 200 years old (as described by their immediate ancestors) was rock dated to be 1.5 million years old.[5] Clearly, the flawed presuppositions that underpin these dating methods cause absurd results.

Rock daters play a little game that makes their work look better than it is. They are briefed by evolutionists regarding the evolutionary level from which the rock to be dated came. For instance, the evolutionist might say, "the rock you are to date comes from deep in the geologic strata, and was formed at a time when fish were evolving into reptiles, say 300 million years ago." The rock dater then will throw out any rock samples that don't show dates near 300 million years. He will then say that the throwaways were bad samples; but you see, he thought the samples were good enough to date, until the results came in, then they became "bad samples."[6]

There is a huge bias toward jibing with fanciful, scientifically baseless, evolutionary and old earth dogma; it's a case of the blind leading the blind. The evolutionist has an old earth view that the rock dater incorporates and uses as an excuse to eliminate the widely varying rock date results that don't conveniently agree with the evolutionists' view of earth history. The fix is in; old earthers have dreamed up a billions-of-year-old earth, and tailored their dating "science" to agree.

CLAIM 8

Animals Evolved Into Other Kinds Of Animals During Millions Of Years

Old earth evolutionists assume a billions-of-years-old earth, then say that the general trend in the geologic strata of simpler organisms' fossils, deep in the older strata becoming more complex (more "evolved") in younger and shallower strata, suggests biological evolution over millions of years. If this were true, there should be transitional fossils. For example, if fish really did evolve into reptiles hundreds of millions of years ago, there should be creatures in the fossil record that are part fish and part reptile.

The evolution of the fish supposedly was gradual, over millions of years; therefore, as the fish's evolution progressed, reptilian features should have increased as the fish features decreased. Fossils allegedly were forming during these millions of years, so we should expect to find fossils of a creature that is part fish and part reptile. However, none have been found.[1]

Hundreds of millions of fossils have been discovered, and none of them are transitional organism fossils. Fish are fish, birds are birds, cattle are cattle, and tyrannosaurus-rexes are tyrannosaurus-rexes in the fossil record. There are no fossils that reflect gradual change from one animal kind into another. Darwinian evolution is bankrupt. "Natural selection" within the animal kinds did and does occur (as discussed in Chapter 14) but kinds (the Biblical term for animal types) do not evolve into new animal kinds.

Genetic mutation is the purported mechanism by which animals evolve into new animals. Radiation and environmental chemicals alter the reproductive genetic make-up of an animal, and these mutated genes are passed on to the animals' offspring, to manifest as slight physical changes. After millions of years, and millions of mutations, a new creature has supposedly evolved. One minor problem: mutations always destroy or merely rearrange genetic information, they never add to, or enhance, genetic make-up.[2] Thus, mutant features in offspring are actually destructive, like dwarfism, immune deficiencies, deformed organs, hemophilia, among others.

The effect of genetic mutation is like the effect a child would have on a disassembled television set which he had "re-assembled;" parts would be destroyed, misplaced, or assembled improperly. Yet, the evolutionist predicts the child would produce a superior television to the original.

Mutant creatures do occasionally respond well to certain habitats. For instance, mutant short-winged bugs on windy islands have greater survivability than their longer winged kin, because gusty winds don't blow them off the islands.[3] This phenomenon is merely happenstance, however, and not a result of Darwinian evolution, as destruction of genetic information has occurred to result in the short wings. Similarly, the webbed feet of polar bears resulted from a mutation, but proved beneficial in the icy polar waters.[4]

Evolutionists want us to believe that fish evolved into reptiles. For this to have happened, there must have been a stage in this evolution where generations of the evolving fish had some fish features and some "evolved" reptilian features. For example, the creature would have fish fins and the "evolved" air breathing system of the reptile. Accordingly, this creature would have had to constantly swim at the surface, in order to stick its head out of the water to gulp air. (The creature would not have been a whale or porpoise which are mammals, not fish, and so allegedly evolved millions of years later from reptiles.) This behavior would necessarily have been suffered by successive generations until enough physical changes (organs for breathing, terrestrial locomotion, and reproduction) had been caused by more mutations to complete the "evolution" into a full reptile.

Imagine a creature, part reptile and part bird (reptiles supposedly evolved into birds), flopping around on the ground for thousands of generations because its front legs had yet to fully evolve into wings. Incidentally, the archaeopteryx (supposedly a "missing link" between reptiles and birds) has been shown to be fully a bird kind (warm-blooded).[5]

Picture a creature, part reptile and part mammal. (Reptiles supposedly evolved into mammals). The mutations which would have been necessary for the alleged development of wombs for non-egg births, and mammary glands for milk production, and organs for warm-bloodedness, would need to have "added" just the right types of genetic information as to induce these complex biological changes simultaneously.

The sequence of fossilized organisms in the geologic strata does indeed generally trend from simpler creatures, in the older and deeper rocks, to more complex creatures in the younger and shallower rocks, but "anomalous" fossils have been discovered that further de-legitimatize Darwinian imaginations.

A fossil fish was discovered in supposed 500-million-year-old rock in China.[6] The scientists were perplexed because that long ago, simple clams, corals, snails and insects were allegedly evolving; the fishes were not to evolve until 100 million years later. The old earthers have no explanation for the appearance of fish "100 million years" too early, from a time when simple one-celled organisms, ostensibly, were evolving into small clams, snails, corals and insects.

Evolutionists also can't explain the "Cambrian explosion:" the sudden appearance of a wide variety of simple creatures (the clams, snails, corals and insects) and, as we have seen, the not so simple creatures (fish) at the bottom, generally, of the sedimentary column. These creatures supposedly evolved from one-celled organisms some 500 million years ago in what is called the Cambrian period, when life forms allegedly began. But there are no transitional forms between one-celled creatures and the wide variety of higher forms (clams, snails, fish, etc.).[7] These higher forms appeared suddenly, with no evolutionary ancestors.

The appearance of the simple marine creatures, deep in the rock column, is portrayed as being the earliest stage of biological evolution, some 500 million years ago. In reality, it marks the early stages of the Great Flood, when bottom dwelling marine creatures were entombed first, then shore animals, then the more mobile and intelligent land creatures. Evolutionary history, reportedly evident in sequential rock strata, is actually the sequence of organism entombments that one would expect from a worldwide flood catastrophe: water creatures first, then shore creatures, and finally mobile land creatures, as the water rose onto, and then covered the continents. (Remember, the mountains rose at the end of the Flood, as discussed in Chapter 4.)

Not surprisingly, the overwhelming majority of fossils are clams, corals, and algae (immobile, ocean-bottom dwellers). As the turbulent Floodwaters ravaged the earth, these creatures were readily engulfed in the mud and sand. "Higher," more mobile kinds of animals were more likely to temporarily evade the Floodwater, and eventually drown, then float, bloat, and decay. This is reflected in the fossil record. Only a very small percentage of the fossils are of reptiles and mammals; the vast majority are of the dense, immobile ocean dwellers that were much more likely to succumb to a surge of Flood sediments. (A plethora of "anomalous" human fossil evidences have been reported by various observers,[8] but are hard to confirm. Nonetheless, only one being valid is another blast to Darwinian evolution's veracity.)

If evolution over millions of years were true, creatures should have disappeared from the face of the earth as they "evolved" into new kinds of creatures. These "evolved" creatures purportedly had a competitive advantage over their evolutionary ancestors, so the ancestors should have died out, as the competitively advantaged, higher life forms, would have dominated. This did not happen. A great majority of orgamism kinds in the fossil record are alive today (some dinosaurs included, as described in Chapter 1).

And "living fossils" have been discovered that were thought to have died out hundreds of millions of years ago, and were considered markers of evolutionary history as reflected in the sedimentary stratum, until they were discovered alive in modern times. (Some of these disruptors of scientific norms are: the tuatara, the coelacanth, the neopilina, the lingula, and the metasequoia whose alleged dates of extinction were respectively 65 million, 65 million, 300 million, 400 million, and 30 millions years ago.[9]) Evolutionary charts were hastily redrawn when these organisms were found alive, much to the embarrassment of Darwinists.

"Evolutionary ancestors" did not die out because of competitive disadvantage, because most of them are still alive today. Extinctions did occur, and do occur, but not because of Darwinian evolution, and not at the high rate through millions of years that is required by the old-earth-Darwinian model.

The term "Lazarus taxa" (Lazarus came back to life when Jesus told him to rise) has been used to describe creatures thought to have become extinct at a point in time, as reflected in their last known appearance in the fossil record, many "millions of years ago," which were subsequently discovered in younger strata. Resultantly, Darwinists were forced to revise their dates of various creatures' extinctions, and thus, their evolutionary timescale.[10]

No transitional creatures, the destructive results of mutations (not constructive "evolution"), "anomalous" fossils, the sudden appearance of a variety of creatures in the Cambrian explosion, and far fewer animal "kinds" extinctions than advertised; all are reasons, in and of themselves, to view old earth-evolution with extreme skepticism. The evidence supporting the notion that creatures evolved into new kinds of creatures over millions of years seems tentative, at best.

CLAIM 9

Earth Crust Movement Has Always Been Slow And Over Millions Of Years

The earth's crust consists of continental crust (less dense granite rock) and oceanic crust (more dense basalt rock). Oceanic crust is slowly diving under continental crust in some areas of the world, is gradually separating from other oceanic crust in other parts of the world, or is pushing against other oceanic crust in some locations. Lighter continental granite-rock crust is pushing against other continental crust in some areas.

Continental crust is comprised of crustal "plates" that are slowly moving on the mantle (the pressurized, semi-molten magma zone between the crust and the earth's core). Heavier oceanic basalt-rock crust is comprised of crustal plates, also moving slowly on the mantle. These crustal plates are like the shell pieces of a well-cracked hard-boiled egg. These "shell pieces" ride on the mantle, some moving away from each other, some pushing against each other, and some diving under others.

Where the oceanic crustal plates are diving under continental crustal plates, the diving plates heat up deep in the mantle, become molten and rise into the continental crust as volcanoes or plutons. (Plutons are magmas, which rose through the crust but didn't break out on the surface; magma is called lava if it breaks through the earth's surface.) Where the oceanic crustal plates are pushing against each other, these compressing ocean plates buckled down, forming the oceanic trenches, which can be up to six miles deep. (Similarly, when continental plates collided they "buckled up," forming mountains.)

And where oceanic plates are separating, lava from the earth's mantle is rising up to replace the separated oceanic crust. When you look at a globe of the earth, these zones of ocean crust separation are evident and look like the seam on a baseball. These rift (separation) zones run essentially north and south in the Atlantic and Pacific Oceans, and run together under

South America and Africa.

Look at a world map and notice how North and South America "jigsaw puzzle" nicely with Europe and Africa, if you slide them together. Old earthers and young earthers agree, the Americas' continental plates are slowly moving away from the European and African continental plates, and these continental plates were once together in a super-continent called Pangea.

The rift zones then began to expand, pushing the Americas away from Europe and Africa in the Atlantic Ocean. In the Pacific, oceanic plates dove under continental plates (forming the "Ring of Fire," a zone of plate "subduction" which created the volcanic activity around the edge of the Pacific), and oceanic plates pushed together to form oceanic trenches, as the Americas and Asia moved toward each other.

Old earthers think this has been happening slowly for millions of years. However, magnetic field phenomena reflected in rocks strongly suggest rapid, runaway plate tectonics (movement), not very long ago.[1] The slow current plate movement is merely a residual effect of the runaway plate movement.

Young earthers and old earthers agree that in the past, the earth's magnetic field fluctuated from magnetic pull toward the North Pole, to magnetic pull toward the South Pole, back toward the North Pole, then South again, etc.; many (scientists disagree on the number) magnetic reversals occurred during the course of the sedimentary rock layers' formations. To the old earther, the first magnetic reversal happened hundreds of millions of years ago, and repeated about every 500 thousand years.[2] Iron-rich minerals that deposited within sedimentary layers oriented toward the magnetic pull of the earth at the time of deposition; so, iron-rich minerals in sediments oriented north many millions of years ago, and then oriented south about 500 thousand years later, faced north 500 thousand years after that, and so on.[3]

Extremely problematic to this theory is the fact that the earth's magnetic field would have been so strong only about 20,000 years ago, that the earth's crust would have melted from internal heat generated by the much higher magnetic field strength. The earth's magnetic field is weakening seven percent every 150 years (this has been measured). Extrapolating this rate of weakening into the past, the earth's magnetic field strength would have been many times greater only 20,000 years ago, and would have generated incredible heat, enough to melt the earth's crust. Therefore, it is impossible that the magnetic reversals occurred over millions of years, but rather within only a short timeframe, within the time it took for the sediments of the Global Flood to be deposited.[4]

This can be proven by the mineral orientations

in lava rocks from the ocean floor along the oceanic plate separation zones (rift zones). This lava material rose up from the mantle and filled in the voids created by the rapidly separating oceanic plates. Lava takes about 15 days to cool into rock, yet several magnetic reversals are reflected in the iron-rich minerals' orientations within the rock. Therefore, ancient magnetic reversals occurred in a matter of days, not thousands of years.[5]

Since the magnetic reversals happened in a matter of days, as evidenced in the lava rocks near the rift zones, we can deduce that the magnetic reversals revealed in the various sedimentary layers on the continents also occurred within a matter of days. Thus, the sedimentary layers were deposited in a matter of days, about 370 days as described in the Biblical account of the Flood, not millions of years. (Corroboratively, the average thickness of the sedimentary column is one mile deep which computes to about six inches per hour of sediment deposition during the year-long Global Flood.)

There are about 50,000 extinct volcanoes in the world today. If most of these volcanoes were 65 to 100 million years old, as advertised by the old earthers, they should long ago have eroded away. (Remember, at current erosion rates all the continents should have been leveled to sea level, by water and wind erosion, within 15 million years.) Therefore, these volcanoes are much younger than 15 million years. Since the volcanoes are very young, most were formed at about the same time, during and after the Flood when the oceanic crustal plates were diving rapidly under the continents, heating and melting within the mantle, and rising up through the continental crust as volcanoes and plutons.

Now, to the "sixty-four thousand dollar question:" where did the Floodwater come from, and where did it go at the close of the Flood? Recall the rift zones that run between the oceanic plates. During the rapid, runaway plate movement of the Flood, water and lava blasted through the rifts, as Pangea quickly separated (at the rift zones) and the oceanic plates of the Pacific dove under the continents at a high rate of speed, like a conveyor belt.

Roughly 70% of volcanic emissions is vapor water;[6] therefore, the lava that blasted forth through rift zones during the Flood was probably about 70% water. This accounted for most of the Floodwater, the rest from forty days of rain (which may have resulted from a meteor's impact in the ocean, as discussed in Chapter 18, and the "fountains of the deep" blasting water supersonically into the stratosphere until the Floodwaters had risen sufficiently as to muffle the blasting height of this subterranean water).

The mountains rose at the close of the Flood (as discussed in Chapter 4): so, say a mile deep pre-Flood ocean (currently the oceans average about two miles deep) could have easily doubled, due to the water and magma venting from the bowels of the earth with forty days of rain, and covered the, say one mile high, pre-Flood continents. In the ancient Chinese's *Book of All Knowledge,* because of man's sin, "the earth fell to pieces and the water in its bosom rushed upwards with violence and overflowed the earth."[7]

At the close of the Flood, the continents thickened due to sedimentary accumulation, continental plate collisions (like the India plate crashed into an Asian plate, forming the Himalayas) and volcanic uplift. Concurrently, the ocean floor sank into the voids left by the vacated water and magma. So, at the close of the Flood, the continents thickened as the ocean floor sank, and the Floodwater slid off into the deepened (currently two miles average depth) ocean basins. This phenomenon is described in the book of Psalms 104:5 from the Bible.

The Teutonic tribes of Scandinavia remember this cataclysm through their folklore:

> "Flames spurted from fissures in the rocks; everywhere there was the hissing of steam. All living things, all plant life were blotted out.

> . . . And now all the rivers, all the seas rose and overflowed. From every side waves lashed against waves. They swelled and boiled and slowly covered all things. The earth sank beneath the sea. . . Then slowly the earth emerged from the waves. Mountains rose anew . . . Men also reappeared. Enclosed in the wood itself of the tree Yggdrasil. . .the ancestors of a future race of men had escaped death."[8]

Remember that the continents would be eroded to sea level, at current erosion rates, within only 15 million years. The eroded land ends up in the ocean, and would have completely filled the two-mile-deep ocean basins with sediment within only 80 million years. And 80 million years is only about 5% of the purported age of the oceans and continental sedimentary rocks; so, within 1.6 billion years (the oceans are said to be at least that old), the oceans should have completely filled with sediment twenty times over. In reality, ocean bottoms have only about 1,000 feet of thickness of loose sediment (most of which accumulated at the close of the Flood, in the deltas);[8] so obviously, sediment has been eroded into the oceans for a short time.[9]

Limestone is the third major type of sedimentary rock, along with sandstone and shale (hardened clay), in the earth's strata. Limestone occurs in distinct layers, and also mixed within the sandstones and shales. It is composed mostly of calcium carbonate ($CaCO_3$), which formed by calcium combining with carbon dioxide (CO_2) in the floodwater. When the water and magma were venting through the rift zones, causing the Flood, profuse amounts of CO_2 also shot from the mantle and began mixing with calcium in the floodwater to form $CaCO_3$ (limestone).

At certain places and times during the Flood, large amounts of $CaCO_3$ formed because of optimum Ca and CO_2 concentrations in the water and optimum water temperature. This high level of limestone formation resulted in thick pure limestone strata within the geologic column. At other places and times during the Flood, sand and clay were depositing along with $CaCO_3$, so the $CaCO_3$ settled to the bottom within these other sedimentary materials and acted as a cementing agent when the sediments dried out after the Flood.

Limestone ($CaCO_3$) is found within most sandstones and shale, thus proving that the layers settled out in Ca and CO_2 laden water, with the calcium having come from massive Flood erosion, and the carbon dioxide having been belched forth through the rift zones during the Flood. This calcium carbonate in sediments set up like cement, greatly assisting lithification (hardening).

The geologic record suggests runaway plate movement during an earth-encompassing flood, a short time ago. The rapid magnetic reversals during the Flood were "frozen in time," as noted in the iron-rich minerals' orientations in lava extrusions and contemporaneously formed sedimentary layers. Rapid and recent cataclysmic flooding best rationalizes the geology and mineralogy of sedimentary deposits, and their recent eroding into the ocean.

CLAIM 10

The Grand Canyon Was Formed Over Millions Of Years

Old earthers propose that the Grand Canyon of Arizona was carved out by the Colorado River as it gradually eroded the sedimentary rock layers of northern Arizona over millions of years. They say that the rock layers were gradually uplifted over millions of years at the same rate that the river eroded down through those rock layers. If the layers did not uplift at that rate, this scenario could not have played out. The grade of the river's descent dictates that the rock layers rise slowly, as the river reciprocally scours into the slowly uplifting rock, for millions of years.

Had the rock layers not uplifted, the thousands of vertical feet of river erosion down through the rock strata would not have occurred. What is the probability that regional rock uplift (presumably caused by plutonic activity from the mantle) would maintain a constant rate for millions of years, the perceived rate necessary to allow this deep canyon's formation? One might conclude a very, very low probability. And if this did in fact occur, why did such a scenario not play out in other parts of the world? This is an absurdly far-fetched scenario, which requires a very unlikely coincidence of the river erosion rate equaling the sedimentary rocks' uplift rate, over an improbably prolonged period of time.

Therefore, another scenario should better describe the development of the Grand Canyon. The canyon, in cross-section, is in a very flat V-shape. Had the river truly eroded the canyon over millions of years, the canyon, in cross-section, should be in a much less flat V-shape, not very much wider than the width of the river. The canyon, however, is about 20 times wider than it should be, according to the old earthers' scheme. Obviously, a surge of water much greater than the river's present flow, must have been the cause of the excavation of this canyon.

Since the sedimentary layers were laid down in one global flood, it is likely that the sedimentary layers were still wet and soft when the surge of water ripped through them. If the layers had been rock hard, the water would not have carved out thousands of vertical feet of canyon depth for about 200 horizontal miles during one catastrophic surge of water. This surge of water had to have been about 10 miles wide in order to have carved out this canyon, much wider than the Colorado River's current flow width.

Thus, a giant body of water, upstream from the canyon, must have been the source of the canyon-carving flow. This huge lake then broke through because of the erosion of a sedimentary barrier or because of an earthquake, or both. Predictably, there is evidence on the rocks of the shoreline of an ancient lake, that covered portions of Utah, Arizona, Colorado and Utah (upstream from the canyon).[1] Old earthers do not associate this massive vanished ancient lake with the formation of the canyon, because to them, the lake formed and then drained out after the Colorado River had supposedly, gradually, eroded out the canyon. They think that the ancient lake either evaporated away, or drained through the already formed canyon.

But the evidence strongly suggests a great water surge (as the lake did not evaporate away, because little of the mineral halite was left on the dry lake bed[2]) through the still-wet and soft sedimentary layers.

Quite apparently, this large body of water upstream from the canyon was a huge puddle that remained after the water slid off the continents at the close of the Flood. In the desert near San Diego, California, within the subsurface geology of the area is a 17,000 feet deep deposit of clay, silt and sand. Since there is no delta at the lower end of the Grand Canyon, the high velocity surge of water that formed the canyon carried the sediments much further downstream than a regular river would have. The surge carried the sediments several hundred miles to the west, near San Diego.[3]

Other evidences on rocks of disappeared "puddles" can be seen in various parts of the world. Also, some "puddles" are still extant, for instance the Great Salt Lake of Utah. This lake is being fed by a limited amount of stream inflow and no outflow, but the evaporation rate of the lake water far exceeds the inflow of water; so now, the lake is in the process of drying up. According to evidence on the rocks of the hills near the lake, it was over 17 times as large and 800 feet deeper several thousand years ago.[4]

Lake Chad, in Africa, is drying up in a likewise manner.[5] These lakes are in basins, so no lake water flows out. Other areas of the world have basins like these, where multiple lakes have dried-up, or are in the process of drying up. The Great Basin of Nevada covers most of the state, and there are hundreds of dried-up lakes therein. Much of the Middle East is a basin with hundreds of dried up lakes, Australia and West Central Asia, also, have huge basins with multiple dried-up lakes.[6] Theses lakes were remnants of the water that covered the globe, deposited sediments, and then retreated into the deepened ocean basins.

It is well known that the desert areas of the world were once much wetter. Photographs taken from satellites reveal ancient lakes and riverbeds under the shifting desert sands of the Sahara and the Middle East.[7] In the desert southwest of America, evidence in packrat middens proves that pigmy conifers and woodland vegetation had abounded in the lower deserts, and Douglas fir trees had flourished in the higher deserts, as far south as Mexico.[8]

The ancient histories of the old Middle Eastern civilizations portray prolific plant life and a much wider variety of animals than in today's Middle East. It is chronicled that Sargon, King of Assyria (about 2000 B.C.) had to hack through jungles flush with wildlife on an expedition in the (now arid) Turkish heartland.[9] Jewish history suggests that the Dead Sea area was a rich agricultural area, "the land of milk and honey." Rock pictures and carvings in the eastern Sahara Desert reveal elephant, hippopotamus, buffalo, giraffe, antelope, rhinoceros, and crocodiles.[10] Some of these crocodiles still survive in isolated and drying-up lakes in the region.

A higher precipitation rate, which resulted from the worldwide effect of the post-Flood Ice Age (and shall be discussed in the next chapter) some 4,300 years ago, enlarged the "puddles" that remained after the Flood. Then, when this precipitation rate decreased to current levels at the end of the Ice Age (about 3,500 years ago), evaporation of this "puddle" water dominated the hydrological dynamics.

As you can see, the evidence points to the recent development of canyons and basin lakes. Millions and millions of years are not required to allow the time for the formation of the features of the earth's surface that we see. In fact, the evidence, both historical and geological, proves the recent development of these features in the aftermath of the Great Flood.

The Havasupai Indians of the Grand Canyon recall the formation of this canyon in the aftermath of the Great Flood in one of their legends:

> "Before there were any people on earth there were two gods. Tochapa of goodness and Hokomata of evil. Tochapa had a daughter named Pu-keh-eh, whom he hoped would become the mother of all living. Hokomata the evil was determined that no such thing should take place, and he covered the world with a

great flood. Tochopa the good felled a great tree and hollowed out the trunk. He placed Pu-keh-eh in the hollowed trunk and when the water rose and flooded the earth she was secure in her improvised boat. Finally the flood waters fell and mountain peaks emerged. Rivers were created; and one of them cut the great gushing fissure which became the Grand Canyon. Pu-keh-eh in her log came to rest on the new earth. She stepped forth and beheld an empty world." [11]

CLAIM 11

The Ice Age Gripped The World From 200,000 To About 10,000 Years Ago

There is much geological evidence to confirm that vast ice sheets once covered portions of northern Europe, northwest Asia and North America,[1] as well as all of Antarctica. The cause of the development of these ice sheets remains a mystery to old earthers; however, they are impressed that the earth must have been colder back then.[2] But this is a fallacious notion because the atmosphere can hold more water molecules (which form snowflakes) when the air temperature is just below water's freezing point, 32^0 F. The polar regions today are technically deserts, as their super cold temperatures minimize snowfall. Therefore, the popular idea of a colder Ice Age climate is groundlessly proponed by both laymen and scientists.

The truths of hydrology dictate that Ice Age winter temperatures actually were warmer than today, much closer to 32^{0} F., as to maximize snowfall amounts in the winter; and in the summer, the temperatures were cooler than today (due to shade from the dense, storm clouds), thus minimizing snowmelt amounts.[3] These conditions were absolutely necessary to achieve massive snow accumulation.

Water enters the atmosphere by water evaporation off the oceans, lakes, and rivers. This evaporated water rises and becomes snow or rain clouds. For the development of the dense and extensive snow clouds of the Ice Age, a higher rate of water evaporation must have been feeding an increasing snow cloud coverage. Since the waters of the Great Flood were from the earth's hot interior, the water that covered the globe and then slid off into the deepened ocean basins was warmer than today, so higher rates of evaporation ensued, which caused more prolific cloud formation.

What could possibly cause warmer winters along with cooler summers? These two conditions seem contradictory; with warmer winters you would expect warmer summers, and vice versa. Since there must have been intense cloud cover during the Ice Age, the winters were warmer because the cloud cover (which was intensified further by volcanic ash being blasted into the atmosphere at the close of the Flood) trapped warm air beneath it; and the summers were cooler because the clouds shielded the earth from the sun. Therefore, massive amounts of snow accumulated in the winter, and little of it melted in the summer.

Currently the average ocean temperature is about 50⁰ F.; young earthers estimate that the Floodwater was about 80⁰ F.[4] The water temperature then gradually decreased through the centuries that followed. This cooling of the post-Flood ocean is reflected in the diminished oxygen isotope concentrations at progressively shallower polar ice pack depths.[5] Less oxy gen 18 isotopes (bonded in water molecules) entered the atmosphere by evaporation from the oceans as time went on because of centuries of post-Flood water cooling. Therefore, less oxygen isotopes accumulated in the Ice Age precipitation as time passed.

Old earthers say that the ocean water has been cooling since the Cretaceous period (about 65 million years ago) when, so they say, the atmosphere and oceans were much warmer, and thus, accommodated abundant dinosaurs and vegetation worldwide. They fail to realize that a warmer Cretaceous ocean would have caused higher evaporation rates and provided conditions for an ice age in the "tropical Cretaceous." Obviously, there was no ice age then, as tropical flora and fauna of the Cretaceous strata (which are really sedimentary deposition from the close of the Flood) are found in rock layers that are just beneath the polar icepacks and tundra.[6] The cooling of the Floodwater is indicated by the decreasing oxygen isotope levels in progressively shallower icepack samples, so the cooling of the oceans occurred during the ice pack build-up, that is, during the Ice Age, just after the Flood.

Since the conditions for the Ice Age were ideal just after the Flood, that is when the icepack began to build. It began right after the Flood, and started to end about 1500 B.C. when the icepacks melted down to their current sizes.[7]

Before the icepack of the Ice Age had reached its maximum range and depth in the several centuries after the Flood, mariners sailed the oceans of the world and made fabulously accurate and detailed maps of land masses before these lands were covered by the snow and ice. These ancient maps were utilized by "Old World" cartographers of the 1500's, whose maps were compilations of these ancient maps.[8]

Precise maps were made of Greenland and Antarctica revealing details of these land areas that were only recently rediscovered through utilization of modern remote sensing devices capable of penetrating the mile-deep ice caps that have covered these land masses since the Ice Age. These maps detail coastlines, riverbeds, mountains, and deserts of pre-Ice Age Antarctica, and the two large islands which constituted pre-Ice Age Greenland. Antarctica wasn't even "discovered" until 1818, and Greenland's dual island geomorphology was "unknown" until the advent of modern remote sensing devices, yet, ancient mariners saw these pre-Ice Age landforms and mapped them with accuracies of latitudes and longitudes that would be envied by modern cartographers.[9]

Partholon, an adventurer of Greek and Egyptian ancestry (eastern Mediterranean area),[10] sailed to Ireland in 1485 B.C., leading the ancestors of the Irish people. (The Formorians, a tribe of giants descended from Ham, were removed from Ireland by Partholon's men). This pioneering group reported three lakes and nine rivers in the land. When a second group arrived in Ireland some 50 years later, they reported that many more lakes and rivers were bursting forth.[11] This was the melting of the Ice Age icepack.

Ancient Vedic literature *(The Venidad)* of India indicates that the Aryan tribes retreated from an ever increasing icepack in the north and migrated south into India, pushing the Dravidian tribes into southern India.[12] This happened in the aftermath of the Great Flood, a flood known to tribes of India, as well the whole world (as discussed in Chapter 5).

Job speaks of brutal icy storms within his part of the world (the Middle East) in the pages of the Bible.[13] Job lived about 2000 B.C. when the Ice Age was at its peak. Remember, Job spoke of dinosaurs living in the land (as referenced in Chapter 1). Quite apparently, the Ice Age occurred after the Flood some 4,000 years ago, when the tribes were spreading away from the Middle East.

With so much of the earth's water tied up in the polar icepacks, sea level was about 200 feet lower than it is today.[14] This is confirmed by the presence of ancient settlements on the sea floor, off the coasts of Lebanon (Yarmuta) and India (Gulf of Cambay), among others.[15]

The sea floor between Siberia and Alaska was dry land during the Ice Age. This submerged land bridge today, between Alaska and Siberia, has remnants of tundra on it. Tundra grows on land; therefore, this current ocean bottom was once dry land.[16] Also, there are underwater canyons that once drained this Bering land bridge while it was exposed during the Ice Age. This land-bridge allowed the migration of people and animals to all of the western hemisphere from the Middle East, where post-Flood civilization began.

The Ice Age had developed in Alaska and Siberia while the Bering land-bridge between them was above sea level. But, a corridor along the ocean shoreline remained clear of snow and ice because of its close proximity to the warm ocean water. So, the people and animals migrated along this ice-free shoreline from Siberia (Asia) to Alaska (Americas).

The highly sophisticated mariners of the post-Flood years were also sailing in this Bering area, as they mapped this land-bridge before it submerged at the end of the Ice Age, and revealed its thousand mile width.[17] (which jibes with the spatial distribution of the currently submerged river drainage canyons on the Bering Sea floor, which were previously noted).

The North Pole currently has a freshwater icepack floating on the salty ocean. As the post-Flood ocean water of the North Pole region cooled down, evaporation lessened, and so cloud generation decreased, and thus facilitated the summer sun's melting of the icepack that was covering the northern parts of the Northern Hemisphere continental landmasses. Coincidentally, this decreased cloud cover lessened the insulation of the earth's atmosphere, so winter temperatures fell, resulting in lessened snowfall. Resultantly, the polar icepack melted prolifically and flowed out into the North Pole ocean, due to warmer summers and colder winters.

This freshwater then froze on the ocean's surface, as this less dense freshwater floated on the denser salt-water. Had the freshwater not massively flowed into the North Pole ocean, this North Pole icepack would not have developed because a slow influx of freshwater, rather than a massive flow, would have gradually mixed with the salt water, and thus, no stratification of the fresh water on top of the salt water .

The circumstances to facilitate the icepack build-up to maximum (probably within several hundred years), then rapid melt-down (perhaps within 50 years) were in place at the end of the Flood.[18] This post-Flood scenario, alone, can rationalize the recent Ice Age. Old earth scientists cannot explain the cause of the Ice Age because much warmer oceans are associated with a warmer climate, as is surmised for the "age of the dinosaurs" (about 65 million years ago). But, it has been demonstrated that a warmer ocean would greatly increase cloud cover and precipitation, and so, according to the laws of hydrology, an Ice Age should have occurred during the tropical "age of the dinosaurs." Without the knowledge that hot water from the "fountains of the deep" burst forth during the Flood, the cause of the Ice Age cannot be deduced.

CLAIM 12

Wooly Mammoths Suffered Extinction Some 10,000 Years Ago In The Ice Age, According To Carbon 14 Dating

Wooly mammoths are found in the shallow layers of tundra and ice in the far North,[1] so they were frozen at the end of the Ice Age (not early in the Ice Age, and so would be deep in the ice). These elephants apparently "died suddenly by drowning or asphyxiation following burial in mud flows, caved-in river bands, or collapsed gully walls."[2] Other mammoths were entombed in pure ice, which is evidently melt-water that flooded out and drowned these mammoths, and the colder post Ice Age weather then froze their flooded-out carcasses.

Most of the pure-ice-entombed creatures are on hillsides along rivers.[3] The massive flood of icepack melt-water surged down these river valleys and drowned the animals, and then, the residual flood-water and sediment froze, entombing the mammoths. This probably occurred in late autumn, when one day, the temperature never rose above freezing; snow, ice, and wind-blown dirt began to cover the frozen carcasses for the winter.

In springtime, further-lessened Ice Age cloud cover caused more arctic conditions, so the entombed wooly mammoths stayed frozen until discovered in modern times. (Remember, reduced cloud cover at the close of the Ice Age induced wider temperature extremes seasonally, as well as daily. Arctic winters became longer and much colder, while summers were shorter.) Many other mammoths were frozen on islands in the arctic waters because the sea level rose about 200 feet due to Ice Age melt-water, thereby isolating high coastal ground as new islands, and the animals froze thereon.[4]

Wooly mammoths supposedly died out about 10,000 years ago, according to carbon 14 dating of carcasses.[5] However, the carbon 14 method is seriously flawed because of the unique atmospheric conditions during the Ice Age.

Radioactive carbon 14 composes a small portion of the carbon atoms that are bonded to oxygen atoms to form the carbon dioxide in our atmosphere. The rest of the carbon, in carbon dioxide, is stable carbon 12. The carbon 14 in the atmosphere is created by ultra-violet radiation from the sun striking atmospheric nitrogen 14 atoms that then change into radioactive carbon 14 atoms, and bond with oxygen, to form a small percentage of carbon dioxide molecules in the world.[6]

Carbon dioxide is ingested and synthesized by plants, which then emit oxygen as a byproduct. When a plant dies, there is a fixed amount of carbon 14 in the plant remains. Over time, this residual radioactive carbon 14 decays and becomes stable nitrogen 14 again. So carbon 14 daters say that the more nitrogen 14 means a greater age for the dead plant tissue.

But the daters assume that the ratio of the relatively few radioactive carbon 14 atoms to the relatively plentiful stable carbon 12 atoms has not changed much in the atmosphere through the centuries; therefore, they can measure the amount of stable nitrogen 14 in the tissue and calculate the time it took for some of the original carbon 14 (^{14}C) to decay into the measured amount of nitrogen 14 (N_{14}). This time would be the age of the plant tissue. (Almost all the ^{14}C in a tissue sample will change to N_{14} within 50,000 years, therefore, sufficient amounts of carbon 14 exist in samples which "reliably" date back to about 30,000 years ago.[7])

The daters really don't know that the ratio of carbon 14 to carbon 12 has not changed much through the centuries, however. In fact, the ratio of carbon 14 to carbon 12 must have been less in the past, for several reasons which cause carbon 14 dates to be too old.

The rampant volcanic activity of the post-Flood years caused tons of stable carbon 12 (C_{12}) to be belched into the skies within carbon dioxide molecules. This additional carbon 12 decreased the ratio of ^{14}C to C_{12}, so plant remains from those years would date older than they really are because there was more carbon 12 in the atmosphere when the plant lived and died than carbon 14 daters have predicated.[8]

Remember, carbon 14 forms in the atmosphere by UV rays from the sun striking nitrogen 14. The dense cloud cover of the early post-Flood centuries inhibited the production of carbon 14 in the lower atmosphere by shielding the earth from the UV radiation that changes N_{14} into ^{14}C. Therefore, the thick cloud cover also lessened the $^{14}C/C_{12}$ ratios; so, plant tissue that lived and died in those centuries would have an artificially old carbon 14 date.

The earth's magnetic field repels some of the ultra-violet (UV) radiation from the sun. So, since the earth's magnetic field was many times stronger several thousand years ago (as discussed in Chapter 9), much more UV radiation was repelled back then which, for yet a third reason, caused less ^{14}C formation.

The quantity of ^{14}C increased through the centuries as the magnetic field strength decreased, and is still increasing, and will reach equilibrium with atmospheric N_{14} in about 30,000 years.[9] This present ^{14}C "catch up," to achieve equilibrium with N_{14}, indicates that the ^{14}C level several thousand years ago was much less than today. Therefore, the $^{14}C/C_{12}$ ratio, thousands of years ago, must have been much lower because of this factor and the other two previously noted. Therefore, greatly exaggerated ^{14}C dates are almost certain for samples from the time of the Ice Age.

Animals eat the plants that contain the radioactive ^{14}C, so these creatures, as well as plants, contain ^{14}C that decays to N_{14} over time. Therefore, animal remains (like the mammoths') can also be carbon 14 dated, and do date excessively old for the same reasons as plant remains.[10]

The mammoths that died in the centuries immediately after the Flood, carbon 14 date excessively old, like the plant material does. The conditions that prevailed in the post-Flood world created a lower $^{14}C/C_{12}$ ratio, so the carcasses date older than they really are. The mammoths actually died about 3,500 years ago, at the melting of the continental icepacks, not 10,000 years ago, like the flawed carbon 14 method indicates. Interestingly, a type of elephant has been identified in Nepal, which has the head shape of the mammoths.[11] Perhaps this is a descendant of the mammoths that survived the end of the Ice Age only 3,500 years ago.

Recall from Chapter 3: wood from a layer of sedimentary rock, commonly thought to be 250 million years old, ^{14}C dated to about 30,000 years old (as the mammoth carcasses do). This suggests that the Flood sedimentation and the entombment of the mammoths occurred at about the same time, about 4,000 years ago, according to all the evidence, after you discount the date exaggeration which is inherent in the carbon 14 dating method.

CLAIM 13

Monkeys Evolved Into Men About 3 Million Years Ago

Some of the most audacious frauds in the history of science were perpetrated in order to provide "evidence" that monkeys (or some unknown monkey ancestor) evolved into humans. The passion some old earthers felt for their evolutionary imaginations led them to manufacture "evidence" of evolution. Some of these proven fraudulent evidences are even still the cornerstone of chapters on evolution in textbooks. The highest heights of intellectual fraud are perpetrated in defense of Darwinism (which is analyzed in Chapter 14).

"Piltdown Man" has been touted as a prime example of a transitional creature, part monkey and part man. However, many years ago it was discovered that an ape jaw had been filed down to fit a human skull; then, plaster casts were made of the fraudulent piece, and were shipped to museums worldwide as proof positive of evolution.[1] Even today, Piltdown Man is presented as being legitimate in some textbooks.

"Nebraska Man" was purportedly a transitional creature between monkeys and humans, until it was determined that the artist's rendition of this "ape-man" was interpreted from a single pig's tooth! From one pig's tooth, "scientists" conjured up a monkey-man.[2] Astonishingly, this Nebraska Man also appears in some textbooks as evidence supporting evolutionary "theory."

Little three foot tall "Lucy" was discovered in Africa, and is said to be a young monkey-woman, an evolutionary transitional creature. She is an ape-like creature with curved femurs (leg bones), like humans have. She is therefore seen as an evolutionary ancestor of humans. The scientists don't consider that tree monkeys have curved femurs like this, so "Lucy" was probably just a chimpanzee.[3] This fossil also is treated as a prime example of evolutionary transition.

"Java Man" is a combination of bones that were discovered fifty feet apart by Eugene Dubois in the 1890's. Java Man is parroted has being a "Homo

Erectus,"[4] but is really from an ape head and human legs that were creatively combined to manufacture a "missing link."[5]

"Neanderthal Man" has been championed as a transitional creature between monkeys and humans. He has thickened brow-ridges, a receded jaw, humped over posture, bow legs, and arms that were thicker than ours. He was short and stocky, a perfect candidate to be a monkey-man.

When Robert Virchnow discovered Neanderthal Man, he theorized that the unusual physical features of the specimen were due to rickets and arthritis. Virchnow thought it was human all along, but merely suffered from a few pathologies. Then old earth evolutionists got hold of the specimen and declared that it was part monkey and part man, and of course, heralded it as the latest "proof" of evolution. However, rickets and arthritis probably caused the bone distortion in Neanderthals because during the Ice Age, after the Flood, the heavy cloud cover shielded the earth from the sun.

Most of the vitamin D we use is generated by UV rays from the sun penetrating our skin. During the extremely cloudy Ice Age, little vitamin D was manufactured in humans, so some of the people suffered from rickets, which distorts bone growth, as evidenced in Neanderthal Man. People in Europe, during the

Industrial Revolution of the 1800's, suffered from rickets because of the near constant cloud cover that formed from the smoke of all the coal burning factories in Europe. Neanderthal Men were people who also didn't get enough vitamin D and, therefore, suffered from rickets.

They were fully human, but disease-ridden and old, Ice Agers.[6] They probably lived well over 100 years, as the Bible says that human life spans decreased rapidly in the ten generations or so after the Flood. Greater ancient human life spans are confirmed by many ancient historians, such as Berosus, Nicolaus, Hesiod, Hecataeus, Mochus, Hieronymus, and Manetho.[7] Extremely old senior citizens often are bent over, and their facial form has changed; this could be a toned-down picture of what helped cause the look of Neanderthals.

If monkeys really did evolve into humans, you would think the old earth evolutionists would have some legitimate evidence of transitional humanoids. All the "proof fossils" of this proposed evolution are frauds, or are grossly misidentified. The desperation of the Darwinists' scramble for legitimacy is certainly mind-boggling.

CLAIM 14

Human "Races" Are Evolving Just As Animal "Species" Are Evolving

The growing popularity of Darwinian evolution in the late 1800's encouraged a mindset that allowed the dehumanization of many people. It was thought that certain people groups were less evolved and not fully human. An African pygmy was displayed with an orangutan in a cage in the Bronx Zoo.[1] The Australian aborigines were thought to be part monkey and part man, and were hunted and killed, like wild game. The white Europeans took the dead bodies to their friendly local taxidermist, then proudly displayed their stuffed people.[2] A popular sentiment in the Civil War South was that blacks had not quite left behind their monkey-like ways, therefore they did not deserve to be treated much better than monkeys. Some Japanese think people with a lot of body hair are part monkey.[3] The societal disruptions resulting from Darwinian philosophy are certainly a product of scientific racism, the scientific "green light" to consider "racial" differences a result of Darwinian, mutation driven, human evolution.

Softening the racist implications of evolutionary theory, the old earth evolutionists allow the impression that since full humans evolved from part monkey and part human creatures over millions of years, only a few benefited from the final random mutation which catapulted those fortunate few into full humanness. So, only a few became fully human, the rest remained a little bit monkey; therefore, these first full humans dominated, and multiplied, and thus passed on their new and fully human genetic make-up to their superior descendants. Thus, evolutionists can say that the "races" are evolving from the original full humans, not from monkey-men.

Nevertheless, the differing characteristics of the various people groups (races) must still be rationalized under the rubric of Darwinian dogma.[4] Therefore, following the logic, some "races" will eventually prove superior to others, and will dominate and multiply, passing on their "superior" genes to their plentiful offspring. Clearly, this toned-down version of human evolution still presumes genetic superiority of some people groups over others (as demonstrated by Darwinists killing aborigines to study them.) Adolph Hitler was privy to this "kinder and gentler" version of evolution;[5] what would he have done with only the original version?

The first full humans, who benefited from the alleged final mutation which catapulted them out of part monkey-ness, were a small group. Thus, the gene pool (pool of genetic variety) of these few humans was small. So, for human diversity (races) to have developed, mutations must have added genetic information to this initial small gene pool. Such is impossible, however, as mutations always destroy or rearrange genetic information, never adding information (as noted in Chapter 8). Mutant creatures (like short-wing bugs on a windy island) occasionally thrive, but only because the mutation is fortuitously beneficial, not because the creatures are "adapting" to a particular environment through genetic enhancement.

Poodle dogs are the end product of selective breeding over multiple generations. The poodles have a smaller gene pool than their wild dog ancestors because the dogs that were bred through the generations were those that showed more characteristics of the envisioned new breed (poodle). The dogs that did not look similar to the envisioned new breed were not bred, so through the breeding generations, genetic information was removed from the gene pool by not breeding the dogs with undesired characteristics. Therefore, the end results of this selective breeding have a much smaller gene pool than their wild dog ancestors. In corollary, because of their limited gene pools, when poodles mate, only poodles result; but wild dogs, because of their larger gene pool, can mate and produce different looking dogs.[6]

Since variety in offspring results from breeding within a relatively large gene pool, could it be that the human "races" developed from ancestors of a larger gene pool? It seems so, in direct contradiction of Darwinian fancy. Poodles, which mate with poodles, have poodle puppies, but wild dogs (mutts) mating together can produce different looking puppies. Analogously, white people who mate with white people have white babies, while mulatto people (part white, part black) who mate with mulatto people can have babies of differing colors. The mulatto people have a larger gene pool than white people, and than black people, so a larger variety of characteristics are possible in their offspring. It does seem that the original humans must have had a large gene pool, so that variety (races) would manifest in subsequent generations. Darwinian theory directly contradicts this dictum of genetic science.[7]

Science Magazine reported that "useless" DNA segments (introns) from men of various parts of the world, surprisingly to Darwinists, have no mutational variation. From this "startling" revelation, it was estimated that humankind has been extant only thousands of years,[8] not a couple of million. Scientists from the University of Oregon Medical School who studied human hemoglobin variation concluded that humanity endured a population bottleneck in the recent past and actually reported that Noah's Flood (with only eight people in the Ark) could have been this historical human population bottleneck.[9]

Could it be that the original cats were of a larger gene pool, like the human Flood survivors and like the original post-Flood dogs (and other animal kinds), as to facilitate isolated, small group, intra-breeding which resulted in smaller gene pools (the so-called species)? The Institute of Greatly Endangered and Rare Species, Myrtle Beach, South Carolina raised a lion and tigress together. Though natural enemies in the wild, they became friends and mated and out popped a "liger" (part lion, part tiger). Since these two types of cats can produce offspring, they necessarily came from common ancestors.

Zebras and donkeys produce "zeedonks," killer whales and dolphins produce "wholphins," camels and llamas produce "camas" and cattle and buffalo produce "cattalo;" all show that the mated pairs are from the same breeding stock; therefore, they had common ancestors, they are of the same "kind."[10] So, all the humans of the world came from a few large gene pool ancestors, all the dogs from a few large gene pool ancestors; the same for the cats, horses and asses, whales and dolphins, cattle, etc. It seems the millions of "species" in the world come from a far less numerous variety of ancestors. This so-called "speciation" (an evolutionists' term) occurs as gene pools diminish, not as gene pools enlarge (as evolutionists intimate).

Some "species," which are of the same animal kind, are reproductively isolated from each other, like zebras and donkeys (zeedonks). They are able to mate and produce offspring (proving they are of common ancestry); however, the offspring are sterile, so cannot breed. Protein imprinting on genetic material, caused by mutations, can effectuate this alteration of reproductive capacity of offspring. Just because similar looking "species" produce sterile offspring does not mean they have disparate ancestors. The genes of one of the "species" were imprinted, so major interbreeding with the other "species" was no longer genetically productive (because interbred offspring were sterile), but intra-breedings within their respective "species" were still practicable.[11] This protein imprinting is one of the mechanisms by which animal kinds divided into various "species," through the generations.

The relatively few original animal kinds (which had large gene pools) reproduced, and their offspring moved away in isolated clans. These clans had smaller gene pools because they carried only a portion of their parents' genetic stock. In isolated breeding groups like these, recessive genes could become dominant genes, and thus, produced new physical characteristics (as in poodle breeding, if you will). Some of these characteristics, such as thick fur, allowed long life for a creature in the north, so it had more offspring than a short hair brother who would freeze at an early age in the cold (Ice Age). The thick fur brother passed his thick fur gene on to his offspring, while the short hair brother died early, having no offspring, and thus, the gene for thick fur would become dominant in cold climates. The opposite applies in warm climates.

Since the offspring clans of the original ancestors inherited only portions of their ancestors' large gene pools, in all probability, one clan would have more genes for thick fur, or shorter legs, or heavily padded paws, etc., than another. Hence, there was a predisposition for the offspring clans to become different looking from the other clans, a built in mechanism for "speciation."

Different behavior and size of the individuals within the respective clans also caused "speciation." Lions and tigers became natural enemies, although they have common ancestors; a cheetah would have a hard time mating with a house cat, as would a Clydesdale horse with a Shetland pony, or a llama with a camel, and so on. The more physically different the clans became, the less likely was their interbreeding.

The climate of the earth was much different after the Great Flood. The Ice Age was developing higher precipitation, both snow and rain (rain in the lower latitudes). And mountains had risen, so there were new ecological zones to which the animals needed to adapt. Some animal characteristics worked well in some areas of the world, and not so well in others. The genes of the successful animals were passed on to their offspring, while the ill-suited animals died off.

When human clans dispersed across the globe, they, too, changed in their physical appearances, as did the various animal kinds' clans, thus, developing the various people groups (races). The unique characteristics of the people groups developed in response to many of the same factors which cause "speciation" in the animal clans.

Genetic pool predisposition for certain traits (resulting from the division of the original genetic pool into the clans' small pools) is evident in the indigenous, light skinned, South Americans. They live in a sunny climate, so are more susceptible to skin cancer because of their light skin; darker-skinned people are better suited in this climate. These light-skinned natives did not adapt to the sunny climate (become, through Darwinian evolution, darker). They had a genetic predisposition for light skin in their early gene pool, so they became light skinned, and just happened to migrate to their sunny environment, where they survive, despite an ill-suited genetic characteristic.

The Summit tribe of Alaska are dark skinned, yet live in a cloudy environment. Dark skin minimizes UV penetration from the sun. UV penetration generates most of our vitamin D, so dark skinned people are ill- suited for cloudy areas because they might suffer rickets. The Summit ancestral genetic pool is predisposed toward dark skin, and they just happened to move to a cloudy environment, and survive there despite their ill-suited skin color.

Remember Neanderthal Man from Chapter 13? He probably was a dark-skinned human who migrated near the Ice Age ice sheet in a very cloudy environment. His dark skin resulted in vitamin D deficiency; thus, his bones thickened and bowed, the symptoms of rickets. The Summits, however, ate a lot of fish, a great source of vitamin D, and thus averted rickets.

Darwinism predicts that animal "species" and human "races," respectively, are evolving divergently through mutations which add information to their gene pools. In reality, the "species" and "races," respectively, have differentiated through genetic variation from the large gene pools of the original ancestors to the smaller pools of the more specialized descendants.

However, the genetic variation between the "races" is surprisingly small. Take any two people, randomly, from the earth's population. The genetic difference between these two is actually less than the average genetic differences between people of the same "race."[12] Therefore, we are one; the human kind biologically branched out (as did the animal kinds) because of differing gene pools in differing climates and terrains, not because of evolution "adapting" creatures to environmental variations through allegedly beneficial mutations over million of years.

CLAIM 15

Noah's Ark Could Not Have Contained The Millions Of "Species" Of Animals

The proposition that all the types of air-breath ing animals were sustained on Noah's Ark is ludicrous to old earth evolutionists. After all, the millions of "species" of animals could never fit on a primitive barge. As shown in the previous chapter, all the "species" developed by gene pool division and by adaptation of certain gene pools to certain environments; thus, the number of original ancestors was much less than millions because their gene pools were large and capable of supplying enough genes for their offspring's highly varied descendants. Therefore, the number of animals on the Ark was much less than the millions of "species."

Creation scientists estimate that only 16,000 animals, from all the animal kinds, could have been the original ancestors of all the millions of current "species."[1] Most of the animals were sheep size or smaller, so 16,000 animals would fill only 15% of the Ark! The Ark was about 440 feet by 80 feet by 45 feet high. "Teenage" dinosaurs and other "teenage" large animals were probably selected to be saved, as they would require less room and food. Additionally, according to Ark feasibility calculations, only 12% of the Ark's volume was required for food storage, and only 9% for water.[2] There was plenty of room to fulfill all the needs of the 16,000 animals and the eight humans who cared for them.

The technology needed to build such a vessel, and efficiently maintain the animals on board, was available to the ancients. Massive warships were built by the Greeks, such as the "Leontifera" around 300 B.C. It had eight levels of oarsmen, with 100 oarsmen per level, making a total of 1,600 oarsmen.[3] Its estimated length is 500-600 feet (bigger than Noah's Ark). The people of Mohenjo-Daro built an elaborate sewer and sanitation system complete with toilets and hot and cold water in northwest India around 2000 B.C.

From about 2000 B.C., Lothal, India had an artificial dock for berthing ships; a trapezoidal shaped basin measuring 600 feet by 100 feet with an inlet and spillway with backing device. It had facilities for loading and unloading cargo. The earliest Chinese showed advanced "joining skills" in their construction of waterside structures.[4]

The ancients utilized almost all the tools of modern carpentry: axes, adzes, hammers, mallets, wedges, chisels, drills, lathes, t-squares, plumb bobs, compasses, planes, and rasps. Almost all modern carpentry techniques were also performed: mortising, tenoning, treenailing, beveling, gluing, and intricate joining and inlaying.[5]

Post-Flood mariners navigated the globe, as evidenced by the intricate maps that reveal pre-Ice Age shorelines and geomorphic features that only recently have been verified by remote sensing through the icepacks of the polar regions (as discussed in Chapter 11). The accuracy of the longitudes and latitudes on these maps necessitates high technological savvy. The recent revelation of such a capability, through the utilization of an instrument for astronomical measurements that consists of a wheel on a cross that is oriented by a plumb bob, shows that the ancients had the know-how to navigate and survey with modern precision. The pyramid builders of earliest Egypt and the ziggurat builders of Assyria, Babylon, the Mayans, and of the Incas, display incredibly advanced engineering acumen, and probably utilized this "Celtic Cross" for their engineering surveys.[6]

There are historical verifications of the Ark's coming aground in eastern Turkey (in the Mountains of Ararat, according to the Bible). The following was written by Josephus, about 2,000 year ago:

> "Now all the writers of barbarian histories make mention of the flood and of this ark; among whom is Berosus the Chaldean (Babylonian); for when he describing the circumstances of the flood, he goes on thus: "It is said there is still some part of the ship in Armenia at the mountain of the Cordyaeans; and that some people carry off pieces of the bitumen, which they take away, and use chiefly as amulets for the averting of mischiefs." Hieronymus the Egyptian, also who wrote the Phoenician Antiquities, and Mnaseas, and a great many more, make mention of the same. Nicolaus of Damascus in his ninety-sixth book, hath a particular relation about them where he speaks thus: "There is a great mountain in Armenia, over Minyas, called Baris, upon which it is reported that many who fled at the time of the Deluge were saved; and that

> one who was carried in an ark came on shore upon the top of it; and that the remains of the timber were a great while preserved. This might be the man about who Moses, the legislator of Jews wrote."[7]

The area of which these ancient historians speak is in current day eastern Turkey, in the "Mountains of Ararat." These pagan historians, having no interest in copying Jewish lore, speak of an historical global flood and an ark, on which the survivors were saved.

A Persian expedition to these mountains around 600 A.D., reported discovering "Varuna's house of clay." Varuna is the Persian and Indian "Noah." This vessel was found in a mudslide and reportedly had many compartments.[8]

Many of the documented 270 tribes of the world that have the global flood legend tell of the survivors floating in a box, or chest, or hallowed out tree, or canoe or boat; all generally descriptive of the same means for flood survival. All the world knows of Noah's Flood, except modern and "enlightened" old earth evolutionists.

The most far-fetched religious fairy-tale to some appears to have much scientific plausibility and historical documentation. Nothing of the Noah's Ark story has been shown to be false, while the geological evidences of a global flood are overwhelming, as are the historical corroborations from ancient pagan chronicles. The logistical requirements for the Ark are satisfied, considering the advanced technologies of the ancients, and the need for only about 16,000 animals on the Ark, not the millions of "species" which, old earthers ignorantly believe, would need have been on the Ark.

CLAIM 16

The Stone Age Began About One Million Years Ago, With The Bronze And Iron Ages Following Much Later

Monkeys began to become human about two million years ago, according to the Darwinists' evolutionary chronology; the monkey-men began to use rocks and wood as tools, and began to stand upright and lose all that nasty ape fur. This scenario is predicated upon a Darwinian worldview, and the reliability of carbon 14 dates for the organic materials associated with "cavemen" from "30,000 years" ago, and younger. (The half-life of ^{14}C is about 5,000 years, so ^{14}C amounts in organic material, over "50,000 years" old, are so small that they are difficult to measure.)

Beyond "30,000 years" ago, old earthers rely on their "transitional fossils" (part monkey, part man, as discussed in Chapter 13) to be reflective of one to two million years of purported evolution by gradual gene pool enhancement through mutations which, according to the Darwinists, resulted in more human characteristics in these more human-like creatures, and thus, extinction for their inferior cousins, the less evolved ones. This is supposedly how full humans evolved and what facilitated the disappearance of the monkey-men.

Most of the "cavemen" (Neanderthal Man and Homo Erectus) remains are located across central and southern Europe, northern Mesopotamia (Middle East) and central Asia.[1] Old earthers associate the Ice Age with the final phases of "human evolution." The "cavemen" (in reality, very old, vitamin D deficient, humans) lived near the southern edge of the Ice Age icepack in the 800 or so years after the Great Flood (beginning about 2400 B.C., as noted in Chapter 11), not during an Ice Age lasting hundreds of thousands of years, as old earthers opine.

These "cavemen," with their crude tools, burial practices, artwork, simple musical instruments and use of fire, apparently lived like humans do in "stone-age" cultures of today.[2] Some people groups have maintained a simple lifestyle for many generations in more remote locations of the world. Either by choice or non-intervention by "civilized," technologically advanced newcomers, these people have cultures which are comparable to "cavemen's." The only large difference is the thickened limbs and facial bones of the "cavemen." As discussed previously, these very old, full humans suffered pathologies (rickets, arthritis) which were associated with the stormy, very cloudy Ice Age climate. They were not evolving humanoids.

Since the Ark landed in the "Mountains of Ararat" (eastern Turkey), and the Ice Age began at that time, one would expect "caveman" fossils to be prevalent in areas at the edge of the icepack, and in areas within range of the mountains of Ararat, as to jibe with only hundreds of years of human migration away from eastern Turkey. That is exactly what the record reflects. Most all the "caveman" fossils are within a few thousand miles of eastern Turkey, and near the edge of the (now greatly diminished) Ice Age icepack.[3]

Some clans, however, like the Toltecs of southern Mexico, had wanderlust, and crossed Asia and the Bering land bridge (as discussed in Chapter 11), entered North America, and headed south to Mexico, arriving there 104 years after the confusion of the languages, and 520 years after the Flood.[4]

Alleged "monkey-men" fossils, which are more ape-like, are found in various parts of the world. They have been shown to be either frauds, or fully monkey fossils (as noted in Chapter 13).

It is significant that few "caveman" fossils were discovered where the great initial civilizations of the post-Flood world once thrived. The areas of ancient Babylon, Egypt and the Harappa Civilization (northwest India where the towns like Mohenjo-Daro had advanced plumbing) are "caveman" free. One might think "caveman" ancestors would have evolved into the technologically advanced builders of these great and earliest civilizations; yet, the caveman fossils are not found at these sites.

After the eight people with the animals came off the Ark and began to repopulate the earth, the clans that retained much knowledge from the pre-Flood world and were more organized and aggressive claimed the best land and began building the highly advanced, earliest cultures. The less effective clans were forced to move out. Progressively, the less technologically and organizationally sophisticated clans were forced farther and farther away, out across Europe and Asia, into desolate and foul Ice Age environments, and to the south and east, as well. They often lived in caves (cheap housing) and made due with simple tools and clothing. As the Ice Age was ending, the pathologies associated with Ice Age environments (and great longevity) diminished. Associatively, the "cavemen's" physical abnormalities also diminished.

The "Bronze Age" actually occurred while this "Stone Age" played out along the Ice Age icepack. The offspring of the Ark survivors, who built the earliest civilizations in the Middle East, had retained metallurgical and mathematical skills. And so, they quickly claimed the mineral deposits in the area and began metal production. The spectacular engineering marvels such as the pyramids of Egypt, the ziggurats (towers) of Babylon, and the advanced plumbing of Harappa were, soon thereafter, amazingly built. These earliest civilizations had technological expertise that would not begin to be matched for a thousand years.

So you see, the more knowledgeable and better organized clans dominated in Mesopotamia, Egypt and Harappa, while the more technologically ignorant and less cohesive clans were forced out into the Ice Age hinterlands, and to the south and east.

Through the centuries, as populations in the advanced civilizations burgeoned, some technologically advanced clans also moved away, in search of less populated areas. Waves of migrations entered the post-Ice Age lands, in which the "cavemen" had barely survived. "Cavemen" were no more because the conditions for the pathologies of these people and their decreasing longevity (in the approximately ten generations after the Flood) were no more.

Near the close of the Ice Age and the concurrent Bronze Age, the tribes from Caucasus Mountains (southwest Russia), just north of Mesopotamia, came upon the method to make iron. The Hittites (descendants of Heth, one of Noah's grandsons) from this area swept down into Canaan (current Israel) about 1500 B.C., in the first iron chariots, and with iron weapons. They had this great military advantage for several centuries, until other tribes acquired the iron-making knowledge.

The Caucasus Mountains were, and still are, mineral rich. This was known to the ancient Babylonians, Greeks, and Egyptians as they traded in this area. Ancient sources say that the area was much richer in timber and wildlife variety than now, and volcanoes were active.[5] Sounds like what is expected at the close of the Flood. High precipitation rates during the Ice Age years resulted in prolific plant and animal life in this now relatively barren part of the world (as noted in Chapter 10). The volcanoes were predictably active because the Flood year's runaway earth plate tectonics (as explained in Chapter 9) had just decelerated, and the earth's crust was adjusting after this tectonic upheaval.

The ancient tribes had legends of the world flood and traced their ancestries back to the Ark survivors and their offspring. The ancient Greeks say their ancestor was Javan,[6] who just happens to have been a grandson of Noah. The Phoenician capital city was Sidon (in current day Lebanon), and Sidon was a great grandson of Noah. Babylon traced their lineage back to their first emperor, Nimrod, who was a great grandson of Noah. Egypt, to this day, is called Misr by Arabs, and the Misraim are listed in the Bible as being of the third generation from Noah. The ancient Assyrians (northern Iran and Iraq, north of Babylon) worshipped their first ancestor, Asshur, and incorporated his name in many of their kings' names (like Puser-Asshur I). He was a grandson of Noah. Africa, to this day, is known as the land of Ham (a son of Noah), and Ethiopia, to this day, is called the land of Kush (a son of Ham).

These nations had no interest in copying Jewish history because they were rivals of Israel. Therefore, their ancestral histories were not copied from Old Testament history, so the Biblical names in their histories are independently coincidental to these same names in the Bible, and thus, provide external corroboration of the names and places in the Bible.

Since these ancient cultures thrived during a wetter Ice Age period (as recorded in history, and confirmed by satellite photographs), it is clear that their founders were the post-Flood offspring of Noah. Some of them moved away to become "stone age" cavemen, some settled the best local land and built the advanced early civilizations (Bronze Age), while others migrated off toward the south and east. Then about 1500 B.C., iron began to be commercially produced, and thus, the advent of the Iron Age.

CLAIM 17

The "Big Bang" Caused The Universe Billions Of Years Ago

Old earthers are usually old universe adherents because they believe the earth and cosmos were formed billions of years ago. They say that since stars are multiple trillions of miles away, billions of years are needed for the starlight to reach us (so we can see the star); therefore, the distant stars and galaxies must be billions of years old. (The forthcoming explanation of a model that superiorly incorporates astronomical observations is gleaned from Dr. Russell Humphrey's book *Starlight and Time.*[1] Please consult it for more details.)

The usual old universe logic is seriously flawed

because it assumes the universe was "formed" from a cosmic explosion, a "Big Bang" that caused matter to expand outward. However, to say "expand outward" necessitates that there is an inward, a center if you will. Therefore, as matter expanded (or is expanding) outward, there remains the center, and therefore, obviously, the edge of the outward expanded (or possibly still expanding) matter, also. Old universers derive this "Big Bang" conclusion from the assumption that the universe is boundless, a direct contradiction of the just stated necessity of a center,[2] and thus, the necessity of an edge of the matter (an edge of the universe), and so, a bounded universe, not boundless.

The Big Bang adherents must use their presupposition of a difficult to imagine (and contradictory), boundless universe, because if they said there is an outward edge of matter (a bounded universe), then they are admitting there is a center. If there is center, there is then the possibility of gravitational influence on the expanding matter, and on the speed of light, and thus, the possibility of much less time than billions of years for starlight to reach us.

A clock at sea level ticks slower than a clock on top of a mountain. This is because of a stronger gravitational pull on the clock at sea level than on the mountaintop clock, which receives less gravitational pull, because it is further away from earth's center of mass. Now suppose the universe is bounded, as the evidence suggests, and has expanded outward from its center. According to Einstein's Theory of General Relativity, gravitational time dilation greatly accelerated rates of star formation (as in aging; that is, clocks ticking faster, away from gravity), and accelerated the speed of light. This notion of acceleration is the opposite of the deceleration of light speed and matter aging, as they approach a theoretical "black hole" (scientists think they actually have located three of these in the universe), where matter and light are being drawn into a gravitational vortex.

There is an expanding invisible gravitation sphere surrounding a black hole; this sphere is called the event horizon. As light and matter are drawn to the black hole, they penetrate the event horizon, at which point the speed of light and rate of aging of matter drastically decrease. As more and more matter penetrates this event horizon, it expands, because the gravitational pull exerted by the black hole increases as it gains matter (mass).

Similarly, if the earth's material density mysteriously halved (thus halving its mass), the mountain top clock would speed up, due to less gravity. (So, the clock would need to descend to a lower location as to slow back down.) In corollary, if the earth's density (mass) were mysteriously doubled, the mountain top clock would slow down because of more gravitational pull on it, so the clock would need to be "expanded out" away from the earth's center for it to speed back up. Therefore, as matter moves away from gravity, it ages (moves toward entropy, randomness), at a greater rate.

This is analogous to what may have happened during the formation of the universe. Matter and light expanded out, so the "white hole" (opposite of black hole) lost mass, and thus, its event horizon collapsed, as more and more matter escaped out past this collapsing event horizon. Therefore, while light speed and matter aging rates drastically decrease when they approach a black hole event horizon, they sped up drastically when they escaped out of the white hole event horizon, during creation. The drastically accelerated speed of light and aging rates continued until the event horizon collapsed to zero, and thus, all matter and light were outside of it, at which point, the speed of light and rate of aging normalized.

As the event horizon collapsed to zero, coalescence of expanded matter caused thermonuclear fusion in the newly formed stars; they aged billions of years, and light from them traveled at greatly accelerated velocities (in accordance with the Einstein's Theory of General Relatively), until the event horizon collapsed to zero. Dr. Russell Humphreys, a renowned astrophysicist who interpolated this white hole theory, predicted the Voyager space probe's measurements of the magnetic fields of the planets Neptune and Uranus.

His predictions were predicated upon his theory that a white hole, at creation, was a ball of water two light years in diameter; at the Creation, God brooded over "the Deep" (deep translates bottomless water), as recorded in Genesis 1:2. Then this water-matter expanded out rapidly, coalesced into stars that aged billions of "earth time" years, sending light at hyperspeed to earth, all in a matter of hours (a few days, as suggested in the Bible). Thermonuclear fusion turned the water-matter into the mineralogy of the planets. The planets' compositions resulted from thermonuclearized water, thus, Humphreys accurately predicted their composition and their magnetic field strength.[3]

According to Einstein's theory, and the high probability that the universe is bounded, the distant stars could have formed and aged billions of years in a matter of hours, and the light from them arrived to earth also in a matter of hours. The starlight did not need billions of years to reach us, because the speed of starlight was ultra-accelerated during the expansion of matter, and the resultant formation of the universe. Thus a theory, from probably the most revered physicist in history, provides an excellent framework with which to explain the development and young age of the universe.

Supernovas are stars that explode, launching debris out into space, in all directions. The longer ago a supernova occurred, the farther away from the explosion point will the star debris have traveled. This ever expanding debris field is called a supernova remnant. If the universe is billions of years old, we should expect many supernova remnants to be of great diameters, as to evidence supernovas that happened millions of years ago. However, all the observed supernova remnants are so small that the supernovas must have exploded only a few thousand years ago, not millions.[4]

If the solar system and the galaxies are truly billions of years old, there should not be any spiral-shaped galaxies. The variable speeds of the stars of these spirals of stars would have caused them to break the spiral formation billions of years ago. The spirals of stars (galaxies) have not dispersed, so the spirals must be young.[5]

Most astrophysicists think that the fire of the sun is heat from thermonuclear conversion of hydrogen into helium. Sub-atomic particles, called neutrinos, are emitted from the sun as this thermonuclear conversion occurs. Some of these neutrinos strike the earth. These neutrino strikes can be measured in cobalt rock. Scientists utilize cobalt to estimate the amount of neutrinos that have emitted from the sun. If the sun is old, many neutrinos have emitted. As it turns out, astonishingly few neutrinos have emitted from the sun because conversion of hydrogen into helium has been going on for a short time, only thousands of years.[6]

The earth is spinning about one second slower every year.[7] At this rate of spin slowdown, only 30 million years ago, the earth would have spun so fast that a day would have been four hours long.

If our solar system is billions of years old, there should be no comets or meteors orbiting within it. The famous the Hale-Bop comet, Haley's comet, and "shooting stars," all these are objects orbiting in our solar system but which should be long gone if the solar system is millions or billions in age. These orbiting entities should have collided with a planet, or come near enough to planets, enough times, to burn up, or reached an escape velocity for ejection from their orbits and been forced out of our solar system. In fact, all of these orbiting objects should have disappeared from our solar system within 10,000 years.[8] (Old earthers and universers say that the mysterious and unobserved "Oort Cloud" somehow re-supplies our solar system with comets.)

The observable evidences absolutely do not require an old universe model to rationalize them. To the contrary, they fit quite nicely within the Biblical framework, as do the geological and biological evidences for a young earth, as well as the anthropological, and cultural evidences discussed later. Nothing in the Bible as been disproved, and corroborating evidences for Biblical inerrancy are abundant.

CLAIM 18

Dinosaurs Died Out 65 Million Years Ago Because Of Volcanoes And / Or Meteor Impacts

Since the orbiting entities (comets and meteors) should have impacted a planet, burned up, or ejected from our solar system within 10,000 years, it is unlikely that they catastrophically pounded the earth 65 million years ago and kicked up suffocating dirt clouds, as to cause dinosaur extinction. Also, if a cosmic bombardment did cause suffocation to the dinosaurs, why were the other animals not killed off? And why did dinosaurs become fossilized in flood sediment, often in fossil graveyards, where hundreds of dinosaurs were mangled and massed together in huge flood deposits?

Suffocated dinosaurs would have died on dry land, been scavenged and degraded, with no sign of the creatures' remains within a matter of months, and thus, no fossil formation. But we have thousands of dinosaur fossils. They were flooded out and entombed in sediment, like the other animals that did not enter the Ark.

If comets and meteors have been hitting the earth for at least 65 million years, we should see evidence of them in the sedimentary rock strata; the meteor craters would have severely dented sedimentary layers, and these huge dents in the sedimentary layers would then have been filled in by subsequent sedimentation from reoccurring ocean encroachments onto the continents. But there are no signs of meteor craters within the sedimentary rock column, which supposedly slowly accumulated during 500 million years.[1] (Meteor craters on the earth's surface are post-Flood.)

There are many meteor craters on the surface of the moon, and very few on the surface of the earth; so either the moon is very much older than the earth (unlikely), or the sedimentary and volcanic rocks of the earth formed after meteor hits on the moon and the earth. (After all, a meteor barrage hitting the moon would likely also hit its near neighbor, the earth). In fact, the only solid planet in the solar system without extensive cratering on it is the earth; therefore, the earth's sedimentary and volcanic rocks must have deposited after almost all the meteor impacts on the planets. Since our solar system is young, almost all the impacts on the planets (including the earth) occurred only thousands of years ago, followed (on earth) by the catastrophic sedimentation and volcanism of Noah's Flood which eroded away and covered the impact craters

Interestingly, Rabbi Rashi stated that a kimah (comet) caused Noah's Flood, as mentioned in the *Talmud*.[2] The ancient Babylonians believed that their god Marduk broke up the planet "Tiamat" (which means water monster) and Tiamat's "eyes" became the sources of the Tigris and Euphrates Rivers (as the Deluge was caused by "Tiamat" impacting the earth), and that half her "skin" was used to "roof up the sky."[3] Interestingly, frozen water is a significant (roughly 20%) component of comets.

Many astrophysicists, such as Tom Van Flandern, think that a planet such as "Tiamat" did exist, at a location between Mars and Jupiter. The orbits in the solar system of the comets and meteors suggest that they came from an explosion at the center of their orbits between Mars and Jupiter. The presence of diamonds in some meteorites suggests they were formed from high temperature and pressure, which would have been the condition in an exploding planet. Comets contain sulfur, olivine, nickel and iron, which are also indicative of debris from an exploded planet.[4] The debris chunks from the explosion of Tiamat moved away in all directions, and then settled into their orbits; some hit the planets, some burned up, some escaped the gravity of the solar system, and others were held within our solar system by gravity affecting their orbit.

The moon and the solid, slow-spinning planets (Mercury, Earth, Venus, and Mars) of our solar system appear to have been hit by meteors from one direction, thus suggesting they were blasted by many debris chunks during a short interval of time, from one direction. The exploded planet ("Tiamat") provides a scientifically valid explanation for this cratering phenomenon,[5] and perhaps caused the tectonic upheaval which induced Noah's Flood, while the other planets were likewise bombarded by explosion debris. Then, the massive erosion from Noah's Flood obliterated signs of the earthly impacts.

The ancient Hindu account of Brahma and his followers has him noting the arrival in the sky of a very small white body which, within an hour, grew to seem as big as an elephant before hitting the earth and causing a worldwide flood. Chinese legends tell how, in the reign of the Emperor Ya-hou, a bright star came from the "Yin" constellation, just before a great planetary upheaval. In ancient Peru, the hero who survived the flood by climbing a mountain did so by accurately plotting the unusual movements of "stars."[6]

Volcanoes formed during and after the Flood because of runaway earth plate movements (as discussed in Chapter 9). The 50,000 "extinct" volcanoes worldwide bear witness to this tectonic upheaval, because new volcanoes are not forming today. Volcanic activity today comes out of pre-existent volcanoes. "Extinct" volcanoes look little different from dormant or active volcanoes. Many of the currently "extinct" volcanoes are known to have erupted in human history.

These volcanoes are young. And recall again, at current erosion rates, the continents would be leveled to sea level within 15 million years. The volcanic mountains, and mountains in general, would be the first to erode, within the 15 million years, because they are steep and often receive inclement weather; so, there is no way that intense volcanic activity gassed the dinosaurs to extinction 65 million years ago, as old earthers propose.

But suppose the dinosaurs actually were killed off by gas and debris from massive volcanism or meteors. They then would have died on land, been scavenged and degraded to nothing within months, and thus, nothing would have been left to be fossilized.

And if dinosaurs did die out this way, why were the other kinds of animals spared? The other kinds of animals, as well as dinosaurs, are found in sedimentary rocks, as fossils (entombed creatures), which were overcome by massive flows of water and mud on the continents by Noah's Flood.

CLAIM 19

The Earth Is Billions Of Years Old And Humanity Is Millions Of Years Old

Old earthers believe that the earth, and even the continents and oceans, are billions of years old. This cannot be, as the continents should have eroded down to sea level within only 15 million years. The oceans have about five times the volume as do the continental rocks that are above sea level. So, the oceans should have been completely filled with sediments within about 80 million years. Therefore, if the oceans and continents are at least 80 million years old, the oceans should be filled with sediment, and the continents should have leveled to sea level, then built back up, five times over. (Or are we to believe that the mountains were once 100 times higher than now, and have eroded down to their current height?) All fossils in the continental rocks should have eroded away within 15 million years of their formation, yet we have fossils and rocks that are allegedly 500 million years old.

The ocean (salt water) has a known concentration of salt. And we can estimate the amount of salt that enters the ocean every year because of erosion off the continents. Presuming zero salt presence in the initial ocean, one calculates that all the salt in the ocean should have accumulated there in only about 62 million years.[1] Yet, the oceans are billions of years old?

Likewise, other minerals are being eroded into the ocean and dissolving in the ocean waters. Concentrations in ocean water of iron, magnesium, copper, nickel, manganese, potassium, among others, have been measured; and at current erosion rates, these concentrations should have been reached in a matter of thousands of years,[2] not the billion plus years that old earthers propose.

Keep in mind that the violent erosion during the Great Flood dislodged multiple tons of minerals into the Floodwater. Therefore, large concentrations of salt and other minerals were already in the post-Flood ocean, so there is absolutely no reason to think that the Flood occurred more than about five thousand years ago. (The Bible suggests the Flood was about 4,400 years ago.)

Radioactive uranium in the rocks decays over time, into stable material (as discussed in Chapter 7), a by-product of which is helium. This helium gas percolates up through the partially porous overlying rock layers, and escapes into the atmosphere. Because we have measured the amount of helium which leaves the rock layers and enters the atmosphere every year, and because we know the concentration of helium in the atmosphere, it has been calculated that all the helium in the atmosphere should have accumulated there within 3 million years,[3] much less time than the old earth scenario predicts for the age of the atmosphere (billions of years).

The earth's magnetic field strength is decreasing at such a high rate that only 20,000 years ago the magnetic field would have been so much greater than it is today, that the earth's crust would have melted. Old earthers maintain that the earth's magnetic field is somehow being rejuvenated (by some mysterious, unknown, magnetism creating mechanism), so its strength hasn't really weakened. But the magnetic field has, in fact, weakened seven percent in the last 150 years (and therefore has decreased 100% over the last 1,400 years).[4]

This magnetic field strength weakening is predictable, according to the second law of thermodynamics which essentially says that all physical systems naturally deteriorate to total entropy (randomness). Radioactive material is decaying, mountains are eroding, organisms age and die, metal corrodes, magnets lose their magnetism, like the earth's magnetic field strength's decrease through the centuries.

The total volume of estimated world coal reserves has the same amount of chemical energy stored as does only 128 years worth of current global plant growth volume.[5] Therefore, global coal deposits should be more than 100 million feet thick (that would keep some hearths glowing) because most coal supposedly began forming about 300 million years ago and has purportedly continued to form through that time frame. Assume that coal layers comprise 1% of the sedimentary rock column; the average depth of the sedimentary rock column is about 5,000 feet; therefore, about 50 feet of it is coal strata. Since 128 years of global plant growth is represented in about 50 feet of average global coal thickness, 300 million years of growth should have provided the biomass for coal beds roughly 115 million feet thick (as 300 million years multiplied by 50 feet/128 years equals 115 million feet).

Now factor in all the additional biomass that would have accumulated from animals dying over 300 million years. Imagine all the animals alive today and multiply their number (trillions) by 300 million years. The resultant total (many zillions) from this hypothetical scenario reflects the massive volume of dead animal matter that should be within sedimentary strata as fossils or carbon deposits (oil, gas). Animals and plants, evidently, have not been living and dying for hundreds of millions of years.

There are, however, plenty of fossils and carbon deposits to fit into the global flood scenario, where animals of a few generations were swept up in floodwater, some were entombed within sediments, and the rest rotted away. Also, the amount of vegetative matter needed to form the amount of coal that we estimate is in the earth today is only about three times the current volume of living vegetative matter worldwide. So, the pre-Flood world should have had about three times the vegetation that we have; not a difficult scenario to imagine, considering the vast barren regions of our post-Flood world that are desert, tundra or arid mountains.[6]

Assume that the first full humans were evolved from ape-men about one million years ago. Today's world population is 6.5 billion, while 2,000 years ago, world population is estimated to have been 250 million people. So, it is fair to say the population of the world would have averaged 10 million people over the one million years since the first "full humans" were supposedly evolved. Assuming a ten million average, 250 billion people should have lived and died during those one million years (assuming a 40-year generation).

Most humans, including "Homo Erectus" and "Neanderthal" men (many of whom allegedly lived more than a million years ago) buried their dead in a ritual position[7], often with their special possessions (flutes,[8] flowers, and art work[9]) Therefore, there should be many more than 250 billion burial sites in the world. Where are they?

Old earthers will admit that the world population was much less, from 2000 B.C. to 1000 B.C., than the roughly 250 million people at the time of Jesus Christ. Therefore, estimates of world populations through history corroborate Biblical history, with repopulation of the world beginning about 2400 B.C., when the eight people and roughly 16,000 air breathing animals came off Noah's Ark (as discussed in Chapter 15).

Assuming the generations after Noah had six offspring per couple (a very conservative number, as people lived from 600 years down to 150 years through the first ten generations after Noah), world population was at least 100,000 people about 200 years after the Flood, and multiple millions of people about 400 years after the Flood (about 2000 B.C.); that is, hundreds of thousands, if not millions of people by the time of the Tower of Babel debacle of Nimrod (2200 B.C.), and certainly millions by Abraham's time (2000 B.C.). Thus, the thriving civilizations of the ancient world were built by millions of people during the 200 to 400 hundred years after the Flood.

The data plainly favors Biblical history over theories that incorporate Darwinian evolution with the notion that the earth is billions of years old. We have been propagandized regarding the "truth" of mainstream earth and biological sciences, but old-earth Darwinian propositions obviously invite colossal statistical nightmares for old earth adherents' constructs of earth history.

CLAIM 20

World History Goes Back Much Further Than "Mythological" Biblical History

Egypt, considered by many to be the world's oldest civilization, is said to have had royal dynasties which began before 3000 B.C. Since the Flood occurred about 2400 B.C. (as deduced by counting the ages of the patriarchs in the Bible), it seems one of these figures is incorrect.

The Egyptian historian, Manetho, who lived around 300 B.C., compiled a list of Egyptian kings that is the cornerstone of mainstream ancient Egyptian chronological studies. However, his list has been shown to be fraught with inaccuracies. The scholar

James H. Breasted wrote that Manetho's list of kings is "a late, careless and uncritical compilation which can be proven wrong from the contemporary monuments in the vast majority of cases, where such monuments have survived."[1] Sir Alan Gardner mocks Manetho's work in saying, "what is proudly advertised as Egyptian history is merely a collection of rags and tatters."[2]

Sir Isaac Newton noted that Manetho reported the same reigns twice under different names, listed kings in the wrong order, corrupted their names, repeated them again and again, and included the names of other great men and women who were only the relations of kings or their viceroys or secretaries of state.[3] Ancient Egypt had regional rulers who controlled various "kingdoms" within Egypt simultaneously. These contemporaneous kings were inaccurately recorded by Manetho in sequential order,[4] therefore, Manetho's list should not trusted, and the timeline for ancient Egypt must be shortened.

The heavy rainfall in Egypt, during the Ice Age, is evidenced by the extensive water erosion of the limestone quarry in which the allegedly 4,500-year-old Sphinx was built, and now rests. But the Ice Age supposedly ended 10,000 years ago? Much heavier rain did water the Middle East and northern Africa in the centuries after the Flood, and thus, caused the intensive limestone weathering of the Sphinx's quarry.[5]

China is said to date back to about 3000 B.C. This date is based upon the flawed carbon 14 results from ancient settlements and the allegedly long "legendary period" of China. One of the legendary heroes named "Yu" engineered a massive land reclamation project. Apparently, a large area was flooded with water, and he organized the project which drained the land of this water. Could this be one of the residual "puddles" from Noah's Flood that was discussed in Chapter 10?

One ancient classic Chinese writing, called the Hikking, tells the story of Fuhi, whom the Chinese consider to be the father of their civilization. This history records that Fuhi, his wife, three sons and three daughters, escaped a great flood. He and his family were the only people left alive on earth. After the great flood they repopulated the world. An ancient temple in China has a wall painting that shows Fuhi's vessel in the raging flood waters. Dolphins are swimming around the boat and a dove with an olive branch in its beak is flying towards it.[6]

Details in this story virtually match the Biblical details, as do details in other flood legends from around the world (which are discussed in Chapter 5). The first solar eclipse ever recorded happened in 2134 B.C. in China, so it appears the "legendary period" in China is not as long as popularly imagined.[7] But, the "stone age" settlements' assumed great antiquity (due to flawed ^{14}C dates) allows old earthers to imagine that the Chinese civilization is older than it really is.

The ancient Babylonians are said to have begun building their impressive structures about 3000 B.C. However, a king of Babylon, Nebuchadnezzar, (who ruled about 500 B.C.) wrote on a plaque that was discovered at the ruins of an ancient tower, that he (Nebuchadnezzar) had refurbished this tower which originally was nearly completed by the first king of Babylon, but could not be completed because the builders could no longer understand one another's spoken words. Nebuchadnezzar further inscripted on the plaque that this first king ruled 42 generations before about 500 B.C.[8] Here an ancient king of Babylon stated that Babylon began about 2200 B.C.!

This time frame fits that presented in the Bible; Nimrod, occultist and rebel against God, was the first king of Babylon, about 200 years after the Flood. At the tower of Babel, God confused the languages, so the clans then could not understand each other, and hence, moved away from Mesopotamia as God had previously commanded, "Go forth and repopulate the world." Legends of this historical event abound from disparate people groups from around the world.[9]

Astronomical records, obtained by Alexander the

Great from the Babylonians, are dated back 1903 years from 331 B.C. The Babylonians told Alexander that Babylon began when the astronomical records began, in 2234 B.C.[10] This is the record of Babylonians, not the possessors of the Old Testament, the Jews. The Babylonians had no interest in historical agreement with their rivals, the Jews. And yet, both nations agree on the time of the founding of Babylon.

According to the fourth century historian Eusebius of Caesarea, Egialeus, the first king in Greece, began his reign in 2089 B.C., 1313 years before the first Olympiad in 776 B.C.[11] Yet, old earthers say Greece and the other civilizations are older than indicated because of faith in the flawed carbon 14 results (as explained in Chapter 12) and their Darwinian philosophy. These results and philosophy have been shown to be doubtful, at best; therefore, we should look hard at the truly solid scientific and historical evidences.

The Byzantine chronicler, Constatinius Manasses, wrote that the Egyptians state lasted 1663 years. If correct, then counting backward from the time that Cambyses, King of Persia, conquered Egypt in 526 B.C., gives us the year 2188 B.C. for the founding of Egypt.[12] Menes, the legendary founder of Egypt, is the Misraim (Hebrew) or Mestre (Greek) of the second generation from Noah. Once again the Biblical timeframe matches.

When the Saxons began to migrate to Britain from the European mainland about 500 A.D., the native Britains (Welsh) noted the barbarous, pagan savagery of their new neighbors. The Saxons practiced ancestor worship (of Odin and Geat), and had no knowledge of the Bible. The Welsh (which ironically means "barbaric foreigner" in Saxon[13]) had been evangelized about 300 years before, so the cold-blooded, pagan lifestyle of the Saxons was appalling to the Welsh.[14]

These "savages" brought with them records of their kings going back to their first king, Noah. These, obviously Biblically ignorant Saxons, compiled their king's list through the centuries, with the Biblical Noah appearing as their first king.[15] We know that the Biblical personages of Noah and the Saxon's second king, Sceaf (corruption of Iafeth or Japheth), were not inserted at the beginning of their king's list, after Saxon christianization, for several reasons. Once they became christianized, the Saxons changed their second king's name to Iafeth or Japheth (as in the Bible) because they realized Sceaf was a corrupted spelling of Japheth, as they read the book of Genesis. They wanted to get it right. And if the king's list was concocted to concur with Genesis ancestries, why did they stop at only two Biblical people to fraudulently insert into their lineage? And why did they report that Sceaf (changed later to Japheth) was born on the Ark,[16] when the Bible clearly states that he helped build the Ark?

There were five Saxon clans that came to England around 500 A.D. These respective clans had their own unique king's lists that converged in the distant past at their common ancestor, Odin. This Odin was worshipped by all the Saxon clans as a deified forefather. The Saxon clans' lists are identical from Odin back to Sceaf (Japheth), and to Noah. These rival clans did not want to have common ancestry with their rival "Houses" (House of Lindsay, House of Kent, House of Mercia, House of Northumbria, House of East Anglica), and yet, they could not deny their common heritage.[17]

The Vikings of Scandinavia also trace their kings back through Odin, Seskef (Japheth), and Noe (Noah). Why would the Saxons and the Vikings, archenemies for centuries, agree to get along and fake their kings' lists, as to have common ancestors and Biblical people as their shared, earliest kings? The Viking's were not evangelized until at least 900 A.D., so the christianized Saxons (evangelized about 500 A.D.) looked with horror at the practices of these barbaric Vikings; no way could these savages from the north have our heritage, thought the Saxons. But they did, no doubt, because they were once united on the European mainland some 2,000 years before.[18]

The Welsh trace their kings all the way back to Noah, as well. Noah's son, Japheth, is listed, as is his grandson Javan; from there, the king's list goes off into strange non-Biblical names of kings or tribes. We know that this list was compiled by Biblically illiterate pagans because the source material is from ancient literature, written in a now extinct language (from before the time of Christ), which was translated into modern languages at several points during the Dark Ages (500-1200 A.D.) [19]

The Miautso tribe of southern China also traces its ancestry back through a son of Japheth, the son of Noah. Whereas the Welsh trace through Japheths' son Javan, the Miautso trace through another of Japheth's (Jah-phu's) sons, Gomer (Gomena). Also within their history are the brothers of Japheth (Jah-phu), Ham (Lo Han) and Shem (Lo Shen). The Miatso seemed to know a lot about the Bible without having even heard of it. Their Noah (Nuah) rode out a catastrophic global flood, released a dove (remember the Chinese wall art?), and landed on the drying land. They trace their lineage even farther back than Noah (Nuah), all the way to the first man, whose name translates "Dirt"[20] (Adam was formed from the earth).

Historians even corroborate this pre-Flood world where the Bible says people lived 800-900 years. The following pagan ancient historians mention much longer life spans in a previous age: Hestiaeus, Mochus, Berosus, Manetho, Hieronymus, Hesiod, Hecataeus, Ephorus, and Nicolaus.[21]

These long life spans were made possible by: a much larger gene pool than had Noah's small group, lower UV radiation in the pre-Flood world caused by possibly higher atmospheric pressure and by stronger earth magnetism (that deflected UV), higher oxygen and carbon dioxide concentrations in the atmosphere (as reflected in Flood sedimentary rocks), and perhaps other factors. After the Flood, the limited gene pool of the eight survivors (the genetic bottleneck theorized by secular geneticists, and noted in Chapter 14) coupled with the diminution of the aforementioned pre-Flood conditions, resulted in progressively diminished life spans during the ten generations, or so, after the Flood.

So you can see that secular history actually corroborates the most accurate history book ever written, the Bible. These pagan tribes, absent the Hebrew account of history, nevertheless had a general knowledge of the Flood and the ensuing genealogies, as related to them by their ancestors, the offspring of Noah's sons.

CLAIM 21

The Book Of Genesis Must Be Mythological Because Moses Began Writing It Only Around 1400 B.C.

Many old earth evolutionist historians say that earliest Biblical history was dreamed up by Moses at least a millennium after the "supposed" Flood, and therefore it cannot be trusted. They think Moses just decided it was time the Jews had a written history and so commenced to create one, utilizing mythology, hearsay, and his own imagination. Thus, the end product should be considered an unreliable, post-dated melange of fibs.

However, there is strong evidence that Moses inherited cuneiform clay tablets that had been owned by his ancestors, and merely edited them, in writing the Book of Genesis.[1] So eyewitness accounts were the source of information for Genesis, not myth, hearsay, and imagination.

Ancient civilizations of Mesopotamia had a writing system, in which symbols were cut into soft clay slabs that subsequently hardened, becoming cuneiform tablets. (The Hebrew word for "to write" is "cut in" or "dig;"[2] therefore, by this ancient means, Hebrews also communicated on cuneiform tablets). After the text on the clay slab was completed, the scribe would cut (write) into the tablet the owner's name and, sometimes, the time and/or circumstance of the text's creation. This inscription, at the end of the text, is called a colophon.[3] The colophon is always at the end of the text in ancient cuneiform tablets.

In the first book of the Bible, Genesis, the phrase "these are the generations of ____" appears eleven times. The Hebrew word for generations is toledot, which means origins or family history. So when the Bible says, "these are the generations of Noah," it means these are the origins, or the family history, of Noah.[4] According to cuneiform writing practice, this phrase was the colophon, at the end of the text, on Noah's cuneiform table; so, everything preceding the colophon was written by Noah, or by Noah's scribe. Therefore, the text on Noah's tablet reflects the origins or family history of Noah.

He recorded his history and his ancestors' history on the tablet, then stated at the bottom, in a colophon, that this is the family history of Noah. His cuneiform tablet covered history from Adam (who also had a tablet, and died about 100 years before Noah's birth), to just before the Flood. Noah's sons, Shem, Ham, and Japheth, collaborated on a cuneiform tablet which covered the details of the Flood.

Thus, the account of human origins was recorded by eye witnesses, and merely transcribed and edited by Moses. We know that Moses edited at least some of the cuneiform tablets, because some place names in Genesis were updated to be recognizable to the Hebrews of 1400 B.C. Moses was careful to use the obsolete place names written centuries before on his ancestors' tablets, and added the contemporaneous place names, as to be known to the Hebrews of 1400 B.C. (Genesis 14:2, 3, 7, 8, 15 and 17).[5]

Moses meticulously documented his sources of information by including, in Genesis (which means "toledot" in Greek), the colophons from the cuneiform tablets of Adam, Noah, the sons of Noah, Terah, Ishmael, Isaac, Esau and Jacob. Thus, Moses utilized these ancestors' contemporaneous accounts of history, from the Creation (about 4000 B.C.) to about 1800 B.C. Interestingly, when Jacob moved to Egypt, he adopted the Egyptian practice of writing on papyrus paper, so the colophon (for cuneiform tablets) was not then utilized by Jacob, but only on his cuneiform tablets which were scribed before his time in Egypt.

In Genesis 2:1, before Adam had been created, the colophon "These are the generations (origins) of the heavens and the earth" appears. Adam had not witnessed the Creation, so this first colophon says "these are the origins of the heaven and the earth," not the origins of Adam. From then on, humans were present to write their own cuneiform records of ongoing history, compile them, and pass them on to Moses.

However, the life of Moses is even thought to be mythological by some skeptics. Ancient historians confirm the existence of Moses. Nicolaus of Damascus wrote:

> "There is a great mountain in Armenia, over Minyas, called Baris, when which it is reported that many who fled at the time of the Deluge were saved; and that one who was carried in an ark came on shore upon the top of it; not that the remains of the timber were a great while preserved. This might be the man about whom Moses, the legislator of the Jews wrote."[6]

Diodorus Siculus wrote that Moses led foreigners out of Egypt because their diseases forced the Egyptians to boot them out.[7] Herodotus and Strabo also referenced the Exodus out of Egypt.[8]

The Exodus of the Jews out of Egypt is further corroborated by the ancient Egyptian historians. Chaeremon and Manetho claim to have obtained their knowledge of the Exodus from Egyptian temple records. These records indicated that the Jews were forced out because they were diseased and practiced animal sacrifice of sacred animals (lambs?).[9]

However, the Biblical account says Egypt was forced to let the Jews flee to the Promised Land (Israel) because of the plagues inflicted upon the Egyptians as a result of Pharaoh's initial unwillingness to let them go. Of course, a great power like Egypt would never admit that they were forced to allow a slave nation its freedom, so they altered their history to make the Jews appear to be the villains.

At the time of the Exodus, the Levites or Cohanim (Cohens of today) were, for marriage purposes, isolated from the rest of the Hebrew tribes in order to be the tribe from which the Hebrew priests, henceforth, would be derived. Sets of genetic markers in the Cohens of today suggest their marital isolation happened 106 generations ago.[10] Presuming a generation is 32 years, the isolation occurred about 1400 B.C.

Joseph, who lived about 400 years before Moses, is also considered to be a fictional person by many Bible skeptics. Joseph was a prisoner in Egypt who later rose to power and convinced the Egyptians that they should store grain for seven years, because seven years of severe famine would surely follow. When the famine came, Joseph did not allow grain to be sold to starving foreigners (Genesis 41: 53-57).

In 1850, the tomb of a rich noblewoman was discovered in Yemen (southern Arabia) that dates from about 1800 B.C. Within this tomb was written that the woman Rajah, daughter of Dzu Shefar, in the name of the God of Hamyar, had sent her steward to Joseph for grain, but the steward did not return. She then sent her handmaid with silver to trade for flour, but no deal. Then she sent the handmaid with gold and pearls, but Joseph did not trade. It was also written in the tomb that the noblewoman thus, was dying of starvation. Once again the Bible is vindicated by strong external corroboration.[11]

Abraham, the Hebrew patriarch of the tenth generation from Noah, lived around 2000 B.C. His life is thought to be mythological by some skeptics, but the evidence of this life is plentiful from sources other than the Bible. The ancient historian Berosus, Nicolaus and Hecataeus mentioned him in their histories.[12]

A fort in the Negev desert (southern Israel) was

refortified by King David in about 1000 B.C., and was named Beersheba. An inscription at the Temple of Amun at Karnak (Luxor) in Egypt reveals the original fort was the Fort of Abraham. The Egyptians, who had no interest in substantiating Jewish history, knew of this man Abraham and the fort he constructed around 2000 B.C.[13] King David, 1,000 years later, may have been unaware that Abraham had built it, but Israel's rival, Egypt, obviously knew of its constructor.

Always, the transcriptions from Moses are vindicated, as more and more archaeological discoveries reveal ancient history. Nothing in the Bible has proven false. The existence of Jericho,[14] Sodom and Gomorrah,[15] and the Hittite nation[16] were once thought to be mythological. Modern archaeology, however, again has vindicated Biblical history.

CLAIM 22

Ancient Chinese Civilization Developed Isolated From Middle East Civilizations

Mainstream anthropologists say that the Chinese, like other people groups, "evolved" from "Stone Age" monkey-men, developing writing along the way, and then recorded their unique history. But is their history so unique? Global flood legends abound from tribes of China, as from tribes from around the world (as discussed in Chapter 5), so, the ancient Chinese were aware of Noah's Flood.

And they were aware of much more Genesis history, as demonstrated in their writing system. They utilized pictographs (simple drawings, like stick figures) to indicate words. The ancient Chinese combined some of these picture words to cause a new picture word. (They increased their written vocabulary by combining pictographs, compounding words, so to speak; and thus, enhanced their ability to communicate, via writing, the ideas they already could communicate orally.)

For instance, the picture word (pictograph) for "boat" was a combination of the pictographs for "people," "vessel" and "eight."[1] The pictographs (we'll call them graphs) for "eight," "united" and "earth," after being combined, became the graph for "total."[2] This graph for "total," after combination with the graph for "water," became the graph for "flood."[3] A total of eight people were united on a boat, during a flood that totally covered the earth. Sounds familiar!

The graph for "three complete persons" combined with the graph for "above" formed the graph for "manifest."[4] Obviously, the Chinese had an ancestral knowledge of the triune nature of God, just as the early Jews knew God as "Elohim" (the suffix "im" denotes plurality), God in three Persons, blessed Trinity.

Apparently, the Chinese had learned about the world's first man, as the graph for "complete person" when combined with the graph for "ground" became the graph for "mature male person." According to the

Bible, Adam was formed from the ground and as a mature person. The Miautso tribe of southern China have an orally transmitted tradition about the first man, "Dirt," whose descendants include Lama and Nuah (the Miautso Noah). The Biblical Lamech (probably the Miautso's Lama) knew both Adam and Noah, so ancient Chinese knowledge about the Creation was probably transmitted through only two people (Lama, then Nuah) and then to Nuah's offspring, some of whom were the earliest Chinese.

"Garden," in Chinese pictography, was depicted as an enclosure with four lines emanating from the center of the enclosure. The Bible speaks of four rivers emanating from the middle of the Garden of Eden.[5] Is this only coincidence, or did China's ancient ancestors learn directly from Noah?

The Biblical notion that God spoke the world into existence is evident in the Chinese graph for "to speak." The graphs for "God" and "earth," when combined, formed the graph for "create," which upon combination with the graph for "mouth," resulted in this graph for "to speak."[6] And the graph for "mouth" combined with the graphs for "text" and "God" made the graph for "to record."[7] Therefore, the ancient Chinese believed their records were inspired by God Himself, and based their writing system upon depictions of Holy history (like those described above).

The Chinese were taught to honor God, as the graph for "house" with the graph for "God" made the graph for "follow, honor, religion."[8] So, the ancient Chinese honored and followed their Creator, and they had good reason to do so.

Adam and Eve disobeyed God in the Garden of Eden, and so caused sin and death to enter Creation. Adam and Eve's nakedness became apparent to the couple after their sin. They were embarrassed and ashamed, and God mercifully tended to them by slaying animals for their skins, and thereby provided pelts to help and cover the first human couple. This instance of God's mercy and kindness to mankind is portrayed in the graph for "depend." This graph was a combination of the graphs for "God" and "clothes" (which is a combination of the graphs for "cover" and "couple").[9] The Chinese knew that to "depend" on God was not fruitless, because He was known to be merciful and helpful, like when He provided "clothes" for the first "couple."

Throughout ancient Chinese history[10] (and Jewish history), the animals offered to God in ritual sacrifices were lambs and oxen. Obviously, the Chinese thought these were pleasing to the Creator. Were the slain animals, which had provided clothes for the first couple, lambs and/or oxen? Abel, a son of Adam and Eve, offered God the best lamb of his flock; and it pleased God. The Chinese concur with this Hebrew notion that lambs were the best sacrifice, as reflected in the graphs which comprised the graph for "deliver (save)." The graph for "hiding place" with the graph for "lamb" made the graph for "deliver."[11] The "lamb" would "deliver."

The significance of the lamb sacrifice waned in the centuries after the Flood. The emperors of China were soon perceived as the main benefactors of God's favor, so the sacrifices became royal events, for the emperors' gain.[12] However, the Border Sacrifice, practiced by the Chinese emperors until 1911 A.D., portrays remnants of the ancestral knowledge of God. It is so foundational to Chinese culture that the brilliant philosopher Confucius (500 B.C.) said of the Border Sacrifice: "He who understands the ceremonies of the sacrifices to Heaven and Earth . . . would find the government of a kingdom as easy as to look into his palm."[13] He also said, "The ceremonies of the celestial and terrestrial sacrifices are those by which men serve ShangDi."[14] This is the Chinese name for the Creator, which is even known today.

The ceremony for these traditional sacrifices has elements of the Garden of Eden story. The sacrifices were offered on the eastern edge of the Chinese empire, where oxen and lambs were sacrificed.[15] (The Hebrews used oxen and lambs.) Adam and Eve were ejected from the Garden at its eastern edge, and later, their son Abel offered a lamb sacrifice, no doubt at Eden's eastern edge ("east of Eden").

"Righteous," in ancient Chinese pictography, was the graph for "I" under the graph for "lamb." It suggests that, I under the lamb am righteous.[16] The Chinese saw salvation in the lamb sacrifices, as well as in the oxen sacrifices (as did the Hebrews). The graphs for "God" and "blood," when combined, became the graph for "Lord."[17] It seems the bloody, sacrificed lamb was symbolic of the "Lord," the "Lamb" of "God." Here is the Gospel message presaged to the ancient Chinese by God through their writing system. How amazing is that?

Genesis 3:15 predicts that the seed of Eve would crush Satan. Seed means offspring; so, a descendant of Eve was destined to destroy Satan. The pictograph for "good" was a combination of the graphs for "seed" and "woman."[18] The "seed" of the "woman," the "good Lamb of God," would "deliver" us from the clutches of Satan. A preacher couldn't say it any better.

The timelessness of God is expressed in these recitations from the Border Sacrifice ceremony: "He [ShangDi] sets fast forever the high heaven, and establishes the solid earth. His government is everlasting."[19] The Chinese realized that God was the Creator and Master of all men, "Of old in the beginning, there was the great chaos, and without form and dark. The five elements [planets] had not begun to revolve, nor the sun and moon to shine. You, O Spiritual Sovereign first divided the grosser parts from the purer. You made heaven. You made earth. You made man. All things with their reproducing power got their being."[20] ShangDi is everlasting and is the Creator of everything that ever existed, or will exist.

So you see, the early Chinese were descendants of Noah and his wife, who in turn were descendants of Adam and Eve. The Chinese people are the same as everyone; we are all descended from Adam and Noah, so, "evolution" of humans, from scientifically implausible "stone age" monkey-men, is a baseless concept.

CLAIM 23

The Old Testament Did Not Miraculously Predict The Messiah's Incarnation

From the time of Adam, about 6,000 years ago, God has promised mankind a Messiah who can undo the damage done in the Garden of Eden because of rebellion. The Messiah (Jesus) is one of three Persons of the Godhead (God); the three are Father, Son, and Holy Spirit. "In the beginning God created the heaven and the earth." Here God describes Himself as One, but later He says, "Let us make man in our image." One of the Biblical names for God is Elohim; the "im" suffix denotes pluralism, so God is saying that He is more than one.

When Satan (ex-Lucifer) seduced Eve and resultantly Adam, physical immortality was removed from the Creation. Elohim, however, mercifully provided spiritual salvation to those who would joyfully anticipate the promised Messiah (the Son) and later to those who would rejoice at His incarnation, death and resurrection. Adam recorded the words of Elohim on a cuneiform tablet (as discussed in Chapter 21), "And I will put enmity between thee and the woman (speaking to Satan), and between thy seed and her seed; it (woman's seed) shall bruise thy head, and thou shalt bruise his heel (Genesis 3:15)." God planned to torment Satan and destroy his plan by incarnating through a woman (mother Mary). Satan would persecute the Messiah and His devotees ("thou shalt bruise his heel"); but Satan's head would be crushed, revealing the ultimate loser. This is one of hundreds of prophecies presaging the Messiah's arrival.

Joseph (a great-grandson of Abraham) wrote (on papyrus paper, as the Hebrews had already learned the ways of Egypt) that "the scepter shall not depart from Judah, nor a lawgiver from between his feet, until Shiloh (Peacemaker) come; and unto him shall the gathering of the people be (Genesis 49:10)." Jesus came from the Tribe of Judah. What are the odds against correctly predicting His tribe? The odds are 1 in 12 (Judah is one of 12 tribes).

About 1,000 years after Joseph, Micah predicted that the Messiah would come from the town of Bethlehem (Micah 5:2). What are the odds of correctly predicting His town of origin? The odds are 1 in 2,000 (as there were roughly 2,000 towns in Israel during Jesus' time). So, what are the odds that these two prophecies would be fulfilled? The odds are 1 in 24,000, because 12 x 2,000 = 24,000.

We will herewith note 15 more prophecies concerning the circumstances of Jesus' incarnation, and compile the mind-boggling odds against their cumulative fulfillment. Keep in mind, cumulative odds are multiplied (i.e. 12 tribes x 2000 towns), not added. Later in this chapter, the impossibility of scribes changing these prophecies to match the particulars of Jesus' incarnation shall be covered.

King David (1000 B.C.) predicted the Messiah would be pierced in His hands and feet (Psalm 22:16). Crucifixion was invented by the Persians 300 years after David. In Jesus' time, the Romans usually bound "criminals" on crosses with rope, not nails. Odds of fulfillment? Conservatively, 1 in 100. So, the cumulative odds against these three prophecies' fulfillments is 1 in 2,400,000 (12 x 2,000 x 100).

David also predicted that He would be betrayed by a friend (Psalm 41:9). Ruthless deceit is historically common against political leaders, but it is rare against religious leaders, so the odds of betrayal (by Judas) are conservatively 1 in 10. Cumulative odds so far are 1 in 24 million (2.4 million x 10 = 24 million).

The Lord spoke through David (Psalm 22:18), and forecasted that the Messiah's garment would be gambled for (as fulfilled when Roman soldiers cast lots to gain Jesus' robe). Of all prisoners executed, what percent of them have their clothes gambled for by the executioners? Conservatively, 1 in 100. Cumulative odds, to this point, are 1 in 2.4 billion.

David foretold (through inspiration by God) that the Messiah's crucified body would not decay (Psalm 16:10). Several people rose from the dead in Biblical history; therefore, let's conservatively call the odds 1 in 10,000. Cumulative odds now are 1 in 10 thousand x 2.4 billion.

Also, in Psalm 34:20 David foretells that none of the Messiah's bones would be broken. The Romans, 1,000 years after King David, broke the legs of crucified prisoners in order to hasten death. When Jesus was crucified, the legs of the crucified prisoners on either side of Him were broken so that they didn't die on the Jewish Sabbath; this was in deference to the customs of the subjugated Hebrews. Jesus "gave up the Ghost" early enough, so His legs needed not to be broken. The odds are perhaps 1 in 20. Cumulative odds now are 1 in 200 thousand x 2.4 billion.

The prophet Amos (about 750 B.C.) predicted darkness would come in the middle of the day on which the Messiah would suffer (Amos 8:9). The pagan historian Thallus noted that midday light went dark in 32 A.D. The Gospels, whose written contents went uncontested by the apostles' contemporaries (Chapter 24), speak of the daylight leaving temporarily on His crucifixion day. Very conservatively, we assign odds of 1 in 1,000 for this happening. Cumulative odds are now 1 in 200 million x 2.4 billion.

Isaiah the prophet (about 720 B.C.) foretold (Isaiah 40:3) of a messenger (John the Baptist) who would prepare the way for the Messiah. Is there any other king in history whose imminent emergence was heralded by a messenger? None come to mind. Conservatively then, the odds of this happening are 1 in 10. Cumulative total now is 1 in 2 billion x 2.4 billion.

Prophet Isaiah also foretold the torture inflicted upon the Messiah (Isaiah 53:5). Most murdered leaders in history were assassinated suddenly, not tortured and killed. So, conservatively, the odds are 1 in 10. Cumulative odds now are 1 in 2 billion x 24 billion.

This prophet predicted the Messiah would be spat upon and beaten (Isaiah 50:6), as fulfilled per Mathew 26:67. Many great leaders have been killed throughout history, but rarely were they ridiculed, spat upon, and beaten before death. Let's say 1 chance in 10.

Cumulative total is now 1 in 2 billion x 240 billion.

In Isaiah 53:7, Jesus' refusal to defend Himself is prophesied. Have we ever heard of a prisoner facing the death penalty refusing a defense of himself? I have not. Hyper-conservatively, the odds of this happening is 1 in 100. Total odds now are 1 in 200 billion x 240 billion.

The Messiah would be executed with common criminals, according to Isaiah 53:12; further indignity here for the Savior. Can you recall any other prominent leader who was executed like, and with, common thieves? Let's say 1 chance in 100. Cumulative odds are currently 1 in 200 billion x 24 trillion.

Isaiah 53:9 foretells the Messiah's burial in a rich man's tomb. The apostle Mathew confirms that Jesus' body was placed in Joseph of Arimathaea's pre-constructed (by presumably hired workers) tomb. In fact, this Joseph himself placed the body in the tomb. Having died ignominiously, what are the odds that His body would be claimed and buried by a rich Jew? Such an act would be viewed by the authorities as supportive of Christ's cause, so we'll use 1 in 100. Cumulative odds are now 1 in 20 trillion x 24 trillion.

The prophet Zechariah (about 520 B.C.) foresaw the Messiah triumphantly entering Jerusalem on a young donkey. One might imagine a great leader arriving on a spirited stallion, not the foal of an ass!

Conservatively, the odds of this one are 1 in 50. The odds total now is 1 in 50 x 20 trillion x 24 trillion.

Zechariah additionally presaged the betrayal of the Messiah for 30 pieces of silver, and the ultimate expenditure of the 30 pieces, to buy a potter's field, to be used as a cemetery for impoverished foreigners (Zechariah 11:12). Let's say the odds are 1 in 10,000 (very conservatively). The cumulative odds are now 1 in 500 thousand x 20 trillion x 24 trillion.

Zechariah also predicted the Messiah would be pierced, in conjunction with being crucified (Zechariah 12:10). He was pierced by a Roman spear, to verify His physical death, according to John 19:34. Jesus had died before expected (as the Romans were not compelled to break His legs, only the legs of the thieves on either side of Him); so the Romans speared Him, no doubt, to make sure He hadn't passed out or faked death. How many seemingly dead crucifixion victims were speared to confirm death? No doubt, not many. Let's say the odds of this spearing is 1 in 100. The total odds are now 1 in 50 million x 20 trillion x 24 trillion. That is about 1 chance in 10 with thirty-two (32) zeros following!

These odds of the 17 prophecies all coming to pass (as they did) is the equivalent of a blind space traveler selecting the only painted grain of sand from a Milky Way galaxy which, hypothetically, was filled full with sand grains. Would you bet your paycheck with those odds? The preceding prophecy analysis (a rephrased excerpt from Grant Jeffrey's book *The Signature of God*[1]) engages only 17 of the 48 specific prophecies relating to the Messiah's incarnation; and there are hundreds of other less specific forecasts in the Old Testament.

So, how do we know that these prophecies were not altered after Jesus' resurrection to match the circumstances of His life? The Dead Sea Scrolls were discovered in the 1940's; all the books of the Old Testament were written in these Scrolls (except the book of Esther)[2]. Experts in language and writing, archaeology, and Jewish history all agree that most of these Scrolls were written between 250 B.C. and 100 B.C.[3] (before Christ). The Scrolls' renderings of the Old Testament are virtually identical to the modern Old Testament, with the few minor differences being attributable to scribal errors. Therefore, it is impossible that the prophecies were deliberately altered. Also, consider the ruckus that would have ensued had "rebellious" Jewish Christians altered the sacred texts to legitimatize their charlatan. Such alteration would not have gone unnoticed.

The Septuagint, the Greek translation of the Old Testament, became popular shortly after Alexander the Great took over Israel about 330 B.C. (before

Christ). This translation would have needed to have been altered also, if the charade were to be pulled off. The Septuagint had spread throughout the Greek-influenced world by the time of Jesus' incarnation; then, how could a cabal of conspirators retrieve all the copies to alter, with the populace being unaware of their enterprise? The implausibility of this having occurred is undeniable.

Since the Old Testament prophecies have remained unaltered through the centuries, we are faced with the obvious reality that Jesus Christ truly is the Messiah. Many Jews of His time understood that these unaltered, meticulously transcribed, Messianic prophecies were being fulfilled in Him. Israel was expecting their Messiah at that precise time. The prophet Daniel (around 550 B.C.) predicted the Messiah would emerge, and be killed, 483 years after the command to rebuild Jerusalem was given (Daniel 9:25-27). (Jerusalem had been destroyed by the Babylonians around 600 B.C.) God caused the Persians to defeat the recalcitrant Babylonians; then, the Persian king Cyrus did give the command to rebuild Jerusalem. And as expected, 483 years later, the Messiah did triumphantly ride into Jerusalem on a young donkey in 32 A.D.

CLAIM 24

Jesus Was Just A Wise And Good Man

Skeptics of the Bible regard Jesus as a wise, "enlightened" and moral teacher, not as Divinity incarnated 2,000 years ago. To them, He was of a line of brilliant people through history who have gifted humanity with moral teaching and noble works, like Confucius, Buddha, Aristotle, Plato, Mohammed, etc., all merely men; but not perfect, totally sinless, God-men. To the skeptics, Jesus and the others were just very good people.

However, should we consider a blatant liar, or a lunatic, to be a great moral teacher? Jesus claimed to be divine, and said that all of Biblical history, including the Great Flood, is completely accurate. The naysayers think that the Flood and many other Old Testament accounts are myths; therefore, they are concluding that Jesus was a liar or a raving lunatic, but not a wise and good man. A "good man" would not knowingly mislead the people by treating myths as facts; and if He unknowingly promulgated "myths" as facts, He should be considered delusional, evil, or psychotic. So, to say He was a good man is a cop-out. He was either a liar, a lunatic, or who He says He is, God incarnated, and now resurrected.

The huge stone that sealed His tomb was rolled away and His physical body disappeared while a unit of Roman guards stood watch.[1] Such dereliction of duty would have been severely dealt with by Roman authorities,[2] therefore, the guards had no incentive to steal Jesus' body.

The Jewish leaders had no incentive to steal His body, and thus kindle speculation that He had resurrected. After all, they conspired with the Romans to have Him executed for claiming to be God, so a faked resurrection would have contradicted their claim that He was not God.

Jesus' disciples did not steal the body because all, except the apostle John, were later killed for preaching that He had indeed risen from the dead.[3] Why would they die for a lie in which they were complicit?

Why would they steal His body, then risk, and actually suffer, persecution by preaching about His faked resurrection?

The Gospels were written between about 50 and 80 A.D.[4] (Jesus was crucified in 32 A.D.) Therefore, many people who had been in Jerusalem while Jesus was there were still alive when the written Gospels were being circulated. None of those people contested the accounts about Jesus, or the quotes and miracles attributed to Him. It is recorded in the Bible that hundreds of people saw Jesus' resurrected body in various locations in Jerusalem. This fact was never disputed by Jesus' contemporaries, who were still living when the written Gospels were being circulated. Thus, the Gospels are historically accurate.

Thallus, a pagan historian from Jesus' time, wrote that a solar eclipse did actually occur in Jerusalem in 32 A.D.[5] (The sky went dark for three hours when Jesus' physical body died on the cross.[6]) However, the Passover (when Christ was crucified) always occurred during a full moon, when solar eclipses are impossible. (Also, solar eclipses last minutes, not three hours.)

Jewish rabbis noted in the Talmud[7] that Jesus really did perform wondrous miracles, but through Satanic power. However, many thousands of the Jews in Jerusalem thought His miracles and words were Divine, knew He had risen from the dead, and believed He was the Messiah[8] who was expected at that time, according to Old Testament prophecies (as explained in Chapter 23).

The Roman historian, Suetonius, wrote in his *Life of Claudius,* "Since the Jews constantly made disturbances at the instigation of Chrestus (Christ), Claudius expelled them from Rome." He also wrote in his "Life of Nero" that "punishment was inflicted on the Christians, a class of men given to a new and wicked superstition."[9]

Another Roman historian, Cornelius Tacitus, wrote in his "Annals" of how Nero tried to blame the great fire of Rome (in 64 A.D.) on the Christians. "Nero" fastened the guilt and inflicted the most exquisite torture on a class hated for their abominations, called Christians by the populace. Chrestus (Christ) suffered the extreme penalty during the reign of Tiberius at the hands of "Pontius Pilatus," and a deadly superstition, thus checked for a moment, again broke out not only in Judea, the first source of evil, but also in the City (Rome).[10]

Cornelius Tacitus seems to have hinted that something happened between Jesus' physical death, and the "deadly superstition" again "breaking out after a brief period of time." Jesus' followers were demoralized after His physical death; they thought all was lost. But when Jesus appeared to, and spoke with, them three days after the Cross, they were energized and began spreading the Good News of Christ's resurrection.

These Roman historians were hostile witnesses to Jesus' life and physical death, and the phenomenon of the rapid growth of His following. They hated Jesus and His followers as threats to Roman hegemony; Jesus and His followers were enemies, and were enemies worthy of note and comment. The Romans and some Jews, no doubt, tried to explain away the miraculous disappearance of Jesus' physical body from the tomb. However, nobody had a motive to steal the body, as discussed previously.

Was Jesus a liar, a lunatic, or God incarnate? The answer must be one of these. The skeptic's notion that Jesus was just a good man cannot be valid because He taught that Noah's Flood was a global catastrophe, in direct contradiction of "good" modern science. Jesus said, "And as it was in the days of Noah, so shall it be also in the days of the Son of Man. They did eat, they drank, they married wives, they were given in marriage, until the day that Noah entered into the Ark and the flood came and destroyed them all" (Luke 7:26-27).

God's destruction of Sodom and Gomorrah is another historical event that is considered to be mythological by "enlightened" modern people. Therefore, anyone who says that the Sodom and Gomorrah episode is part of true history must be lying, or delusional. However, Jesus said:

> "Likewise as it was in the days of Lot; they did eat, they drank, they bought, they sold, they planted, they builded; but the same day that Lot went out of Sodom it rained fire and brimstone of heaven, and destroyed them all. Even thus shall it be in the day when the Son of man is revealed" (Luke 7:28-30).

Unbeknownst to most people, modern discoveries of ancient written records (Ebla tablets)[8] confirm the historicity of these cities.[11]

Good men do not deliberately perpetuate lies, only liars or fools do. Thus, Jesus was not just a wise and good man; he was a liar, or a lunatic, or God incarnate. Based on the evidence, the correct answer is not difficult to deduce.

CLAIM 25

The Bible Now Has No Predictive Power Regarding Our Future

We have seen how the Old Testament prophecies supernaturally describe Jesus' incarnation, in great detail, hundreds of years before He physically appeared on earth. And we have seen how the Gospel accounts of Jesus' life went unchallenged by His contemporaries; so apparently, He is infallible. Jesus said, "But as the days of Noah were, so shall also the coming of the Son of man be. For as in the days that were before the flood they were eating, and drinking, marrying and giving in marriage, until the day that Noah entered into the ark, and knew not until the flood came, and took them all away; so shall also the coming of the Son of man be" (Matthew 24:37).

Noah had warned the people of their unrighteousness, but they repented not, and were destroyed. But there will not be global destruction by water again , as God promised by the sign of the rainbow (Genesis 9:13). The future destruction of the unrighteous is detailed in the book of Revelation.

Jesus was predicted by the prophets, but can He predict? He foresaw the destruction of the Temple in Jerusalem, and even stated that not a stone of the Temple would go unturned.[1] In 70 A.D., the Romans laid waste to Jerusalem, and burned the Temple. The gold of the Temple melted in the fire and dripped down between the stone blocks, so the Romans overturned the blocks to retrieve the gold.[2] Prophecy fulfilled.

Regarding the Temple's destruction, Jesus presciently said, "Behold, your house (Temple) is left unto you desolate. For I say unto you, Ye shall not see me henceforth, till ye shall say, Blessed is he that cometh in the name of the Lord."[3] The Messiah is referring to a future time when the world behaves as "in the days of Noah," in defiant rebellion before the Lord, and thus, the battle of Armageddon ensues, and Christ shall be welcomed as the true Messiah. Jesus is talking about a more distant time when Jews, after the destruction of Jerusalem and the Diaspora (global migrations of Jews), would subsequently regroup in the Holy Land.[4] The modern state of Israel was established in 1948, defying all odds. How many nations, destroyed thousands of years ago, have reconstituted under the same banner as before? The likelihood of a modern Israel forming is like that of a modern Phoenicia, or a modern Thrace.

Jews have usually intra-married, through the generations after the Messiah's incarnation, as they had before; so they have not fully assimilated into the more dominant societies that hosted them in the centuries after Jerusalem's fall. Thus, they retained their "Israeli-ness." Who today says, "I'm a Phoenician!" or "I'm a Thracian!" Few, if any, do. But Israelis are back in the Holy Land, as predicted by Jesus.

God calls the Holy Land Israel, yet many today insist on naming it after a long ago vanquished enemy of Israel's, the Philistines (descendants of Ham, through Misraim[5]). The Philistines were a major threat to the Israelis from about 1300 to 600 B.C.[6] David's giant victim, Goliath, was a Philistine. David subdued them, and they virtually disappeared from the pages of history. However, about 330 B.C., the new conquerors of the Holy Land, Greece, revived the memory of the defeated, non-existent Philistine nation by rudely naming the Land "Palestine."[7] The

Greeks were notorious for ignoring ancestral names of peoples and places, and renaming them to their own liking, as to obscure the historical roots of rival nations.[8] To this day, many refer to the Holy Land as Palestine (Philistine), and thus knowingly, or unknowingly, mock God's plan.

The Jews have maintained their genealogical and cultural integrity through the centuries because they have faith that the Messiah will come (in reality, come back) to Jerusalem. Through the centuries, they repeated to each other, "next year in Jerusalem." That "next year" came in 1967, when Jerusalem was secured by Israel. Jews always had confidence that God would re-gather them to the Holy Land, as the inspired Old Testament prophet, Isaiah, foresaw: "And He (God) will set up an ensign for the nations, and shall assemble the outcasts of Israel , and gather together the dispersed of Judah from the four corners of the earth."[9] The Jews have always known that they belong in Israel, and now they are there to stay.

Jesus predicted that His Gospel would be preached in all the world, and then, the end of the age would come.[10] Numbering in the hundreds at that time, His followers must have been shocked in hearing that His message would be preached to every nation on earth. "All powerful Rome" was ruthlessly eliminating dissidents to their hegemony, so global dissemination of the Gospel and its "Kingdom of God" concepts must have been impossible to imagine. And predictably, Rome did execute many thousands of Christians in the ensuing years, and thus unintentionally fanned the flames of dedication to world evangelism.

Today the Good News of Jesus Christ is presented to almost all the nations by missionaries, satellite and land-based television and radio, literature, and "one on one" evangelism. The Gospel soon will have been preached in all the world, as He predicted. Christ's apostle John (Revelation 11:7-12) was inspired to write that two witnesses would preach and perform miracles in Jerusalem, and be killed; then, their dead bodies would be seen in the street for three-and-one-half days until they will come to life and ascend to Heaven.

According to the prophecy, all the world will see the two bodies lying in the street. "All the world will see?" The people of Roman times must have considered that impossible. Ah, but the apostle obviously sensed a future marvel that would allow all the world to view their bodies (television)! It is unfathomable to even dream that a mere mortal in Roman times could foresee such a technological capability. John wrote Revelation around 80 A.D., but had a supernatural vision of the technologies that would be available to mankind 2,000 years in the future. Only God

Almighty could inspire like that.

Jesus incarnated 2,000 years ago, Abraham lived 2,000 years before that, and Adam and Eve 2,000 years before that; about 6,000 years, total. God says that a "thousand years to Him is as a day."[11] So, since He created everything in six days, then rested, might the creation similarly rest after 6,000 years? Jesus spoke of a time when "the lamb will lay down with the lion, and swords will be beaten into plowshares;"[12] that will be after Armageddon when Jesus will rule on earth for 1,000 years.[13] One thousand years of rest for the creation, following 6,000 years of human rule (often guided by Satan and his minions); it does seem that we are near Christ's reign on earth.

The Old Testament (Ezekiel 38, 39) predicts that specific countries surrounding Israel will attack her, and be miraculously defeated, leaving a gruesome battlefield that will take seven years to clean up. The anti-Christ will emerge just after this God-caused victory for Israel, promising peace, and a false world religion. He will rule for seven years, until all the world comes against Israel at the battle of Armageddon, and Jesus Christ defeats the world's armies, and so begins His 1,000-year reign. Sometime during this seven year "tribulation period," believers in Jesus the Messiah will be "raptured," in the "twinkling of an eye," they will be changed (1 Corinthians 15:52).

As the anti-Christ comes to power, the Israelis, knowing that God caused their amazing victory (as predicted 2,500 years before), will rebuild the Temple, and re-institute animal sacrifices to Elohim (as discussed in Chapter 22). The anti-Christ will tolerate the Jewish rituals until three-and-one-half years into his seven-year reign, when he will take control of the Temple, end the sacrifices, and begin a three-and-one-half year reign of Satanic fury,[14] ending at Armageddon where "the seed of the woman (Jesus)" will all but end Satan's influence on earth. (Satan will be allowed a little time to do his thing at the end of Jesus' thousand-year reign on this earth. Then, Satan and his followers will be put away forever, as God burns up the first creation, and makes a new heaven and earth in which His followers will dwell with Him.[15])

Abraham, about 400 years after the Flood, was promised that through his seed, all the nations of the world would be blessed; Jesus is that seed. The Jews know that the Messiah will come, but most aren't aware that He will be returning. When they rebuild the Temple and begin to slaughter lambs to God, most will have no idea that Jesus, the Lamb of God, had caused their great military victory (predicted by Ezekiel), and would soon come to lead them, and rule the world. Most won't see that the Gospel of Jesus Christ, preached in all the world, is a fulfillment of

God's promise to Abraham; that through his seed, all the nations would be blessed.

Many Jews have believed in Jesus through the centuries, but most have not. God blinded their spiritual eyes, so that the Gentile nations would be blessed.[16] The time of the Gentiles is almost over, and God will intervene more intensely for Israel in the near future, to overcome the anti-Christ.

Jesus successfully predicted the overturning of the Temple's stones, and the improbable reformation of Israel; so, should we pay attention to this Prophet, and the other prophets? They have never been wrong, how could you not put stock in the prophecies of the Bible? Our futures are laid out on its pages, but who is wise enough to heed?

Epilogue

Humans would never invent a God (like Elohim) who is capable of condemning them to eternal damnation. After all, why would a person dream up a God who would mete out intense and eternal judgment on much of humankind, and maybe even on himself? No, a righteous God, who judges the unrighteous, is an unsettling notion to those of us who are well aware of our own flaws and failures.

A religion more likely to be appreciated by humans is one in which there is no Creator to Whom one must answer, and one in which humans are randomly evolved from a primeval watery chaos and are the masters of their own destinies. Satan and his minions then can tell them they are correct in their assessment of life, and so, they are free to do as they please without fear of punishment.

Strangely, Satan probably thinks that he, too, is not a created being; after all, why would he have rebelled against an entity that he knew to be the vastly superior Creator of all, and thus certainly suffer eternal defeat? Could it be that Satan thought that both he and God evolved from pre-existent primordial waters, and so are similar beings? Perhaps Satan didn't believe that God actually created the waters (Genesis 1:1-2) from which Satan thought they both had evolved. Old earth evolution is, no doubt, a device used by the enemies of God to convince humankind that the Bible is mythology, and therefore, that the idea of a righteous Creator is unscientific and baseless.

The battle has been raging for the hearts and minds of men since the Garden of Eden. Satan wants to bring as many into his kingdom as possible, so he requires that we call God a liar by accepting false beliefs, like the posit that all life (including his and God's) evolved out of a pre-existent watery chaos. Satan is saying, "God evolved, I evolved, and you too evolved, so we are all as gods; now do as you please." Our fallen natures love the sound of "do your own thing, you'll not be judged." And yet, your conscience tells you that Satan is a liar. And so you might ask, "how do I respond to this inner awareness?"

The evidence is overwhelming that all of the Bible is true; therefore, you have no excuse. The Gospel is being preached in all the world, and millions are being saved from eternal torment by simply, yet sincerely, asking Jesus to forgive them of their sins and to help them. It can happen for you right now. I pray it does, as salvation is indescribably liberating and peaceful, when you are secure in the knowledge that you will forever be an adopted child of God Almighty. May the gift of salvation, offered freely by the Prince of Peace, be yours today. We are not guaranteed tomorrow, today is the day of salvation.

End Notes

Chapter 1

1. Bill Cooper, *After The Flood* (West Sussex, England: New Wine Press, 1995), 131.
2. Ibid., 133.
3. Ibid., 141.
4. Ibid., 133.
5. "The Life of Apollonius of Tyana by Philostratus," http://www.magna.com.au/~prfbrown/atyana25.html
6. Ibid.
7. Pliny the Elder, *Naturalis Historia*, Eighth Book, Chapters 11, 12.
8. "Dragons in History," http://www.genesispark.com/genpark/history/history.htm
9. Perle S. Epstein, *Monsters: Their Histories, Homes and Habits* (Garden City, New York: Doubleday, 1973), 43.
10. "African Pterodactyls," M.D.W. Jeffreys http://www.herper.com/AFpterodactyls.html
11. Bill Johnson, "Thunderbirds: Did the American Indians See Winged Dinosaurs?," Creation Ex Nihilo, vol. 24, no. 2 (2002): 28.
12. Duane T. Gish, *Dinosaurs by Design* (Green Forest, Arkansas: Master Books, 1992), 16.

13. "Dragons in History"
14. Conrad Gesner, Historia Animalium, 1551-1587 A.D., 224.
15. "Evidence that Humans and Dinosaurs Lived at the Same Time," http://www.creationists.org/dinos_artifacts_and_art.html
16. "Ancient Rock is Still A Mystery," http://www.desertusa.com/mag99/aug/stories/rocks.html
17. Johnson, "Thunderbirds," 29.
18. "A Living Dinosaur?," Creation Ex Nihilo, vol. 23, No. 1 (2001): (back cover).
19. Timofey Alferov, "Dragons, Animals . . . Not Apparitions," Creation Ex Nihilo, vol. 22, no. 3 (2001): 16.

Chapter 2

1. Gerard Muyzer, Geology, vol. 20, Oct. 1992.
2. Ariel A. Roth, *Origins* (Hagerstown, Maryland: Review and Herald Publishing Association, 1998), 242.
3. Ibid., 243.
4. Carl Wieland, "Sensational Dinosaur Blood Report!," Creation Ex Nihilo, vol. 19, no. 4, (1997): 42.
5. Philip J. Currie and Eva B. Koppelus, *101 Questions About Dinosaurs* (Mineola, New York: Dover Publications, 1996), 12.
6. Buddy Davis, Mike Liston, and John Whitmore, *The Great Dinosaur Adventure* (Green Forest, Arkansas: Master Books, 1998), 88.
   and
   M. Helder, "Fresh Dinosaur Bones Found," Creation Ex Nihilo, vol. 20, no. 4, (1992): 16.
7. Carl Wieland, "Dinosaur Bones, Just How Old Are They Really?," Creation Ex Nihilo, vol. 21, no. 1, (1999): 55.

Chapter 3

1. Ariel A. Roth, *Origins: Linking Science and Scripture* (Hagerstown, Maryland: Review and Herald Publishing Association, 1998), 218-219.
2. John D. Morris, *The Young Earth* (Green Forest, Arkansas: Master Books, 1994), 100.
3. G.S. McLean, Roger Oakland, and Larry McLean, *The Evidence For Creation* (Springdale, Pennsylvania: Whitaker House, 1989), 167.
4. Henry M. Morris, *Scientific Creationism* (Green Forest, Arkansas: Master Books, 1999), 97-100.
5. Dennis Gordon Lindsay, *The Birth of Planet Earth and the Age of the Universe* (Dallas, Texas: Christ For The Nations, 1993), 18-20.
6. Alexander V Lalomov, "Fossil Reptiles on the Russian Platform," Technical Journal (Answers in Genesis, Florence, Kentucky), vol. 15, no. 1, 6-7.
7. Morris, *The Young Earth*, 88-90.
8. Roth, *Origins*, 218.

Chapter 4

1. John D. Morris, *The Young Earth* (Green Forest, Arkansas: Master Books, 1994), 106-109.
2. Ibid., 107.
3. Ariel A. Roth, *Origins: Linking Science and Scripture* (Hagerstown, Maryland: Review and Herald Publishing Association, 1998), 264.

Chapter 5

1. Sir James Frazer, *Folklore in the Old Testament* (London, England: Macmillan and Company, 1918), 237.
2. Ariel A. Roth, *Origins: Linking Science and Scripture* (Hagerstown, Maryland: Review and Herald Publishing Association, 1998), 306.
3. Flood Stories from Around the World, http://www.best.com/~atta/floods.htm
4. Ibid.
5. Ibid.
6. Ibid.
7. Ibid.
8. Ibid.
9. Ibid.
10. Ibid.
11. Ibid.
12. Ibid.

Chapter 6

1. G.S. McLean, Roger Oakland, and Larry McLean, *The Evidence For Creation* (Eston, Saskatchewan: Full Gospel Bible Institute, 1989), 33.
2. R. M. Kosanke, "Palynological Studies of the Coals of the Princess Reserve District in Northeastern Kentucky," U.S. Geological Survey Professional Paper no. 839, (1973): 20.
3. Andrew Snelling, "Coal Beds and Noah's Flood," Creation Ex Nihilo, vol. 8, no. 3, (1986): 20-21.
4. Stuart E. Nevins, "The Origin of Coal," Impact Article

No. 41, Institute For Creation Research, El Cajon, California.

5. Andrew Snelling, "Stumping Old Age Dogma," Creation Ex Nihilo, vol. 8, no. 3, (1986): 20-21.
6. Paul Giem, "Carbon 14 Content of Fossil Carbon," Geoscience Research Institute, Loma Linda, California, http://www.grisda.org/origins/51006.htm
7. N.A. Rupke, "Sedimentary Evidence For The Allochthonous Origin Of Stigmaria, Carboniferous, Nova Scotia," Geological Society of America Bulletin, vol. 80. (1969): 2109-2114.
8. Henry M. Morris, *Scientific Creationism* (Green Forest, Arkansas: Master Books, 1998), 108.
9. Tas Walker, "Coal, Memorial to the Flood," Creation Ex Nihilo, vol. 23, no. 2, (2001): 26.
10. "Oil In Minutes," Creation Ex Nihilo, vol. 19, no. 3, (1997): 9.

Chapter 7

1. John D. Morris, *The Young Earth* (Green Forest, Arkansas: Master Books, 1999), 53.
2. "Dating Doubt," Creation Ex Nihilo, vol.22, no. 2, (2000): 9.
3. Morris, *The Young Earth*, 53.
4. Keith Swenson, "Radio-Dating In Rubble," Creation Ex Nihilo, vol. 23, no. 3, (2001): 23-25.
5. Ibid. 24.
6. John Woodmorappe, "Radiometric Geochronology Reappraised," Creation Research Quarterly, vol. 16, no. 2, (1979): 102-148.

Chapter 8

1. Duane T. Gish, *Evolution: The Fossils Still Say No!* (El Cajon, California: Institute For Creation Research, 1995), 41.
2. Lane Lester, "Genetics: No Friend of Evolution," Creation Ex Nihilo, vol. 20., no. 2, (1998): 22.
3. Ibid., 22.
4. Paula Weston and Carl Wieland, "Bears Across the World," Creation Ex Nihilo, vol. 20, no. 4, (1998): 30.
5. Henry M. Morris, *Scientific Creationism* (Green Forest, Arkansas: Master Books 1998), 85.
6. D. Shu, et. al. "Lower Cambrian Vertebrates From South China," Nature 402 (6765) (1999): 42-46.
7. Gish, *Evolution*, 53.
8. Michael and Richard L. Thompson, *Forbidden Archeology* (Los Angeles, California: Bhaktivedanta Book Publishing, Inc., 1996.
9. Henry M. Morris, *Scientific Creationism*, 89.
10. "Mass Extinction Doubts," Creation Ex Nihilo, vol. 24, no. 2, (2002): 8.

Chapter 9

1. Russell Humphreys, "Evidence for a Young World," http://www.rae.org/yworld.htm
2. John Woodmorappe, *The Mythology of Modern Dating Methods* (El Cajon, California: Institute for Creation Research, 1999), 54.
3. J.W. Holt and J.L. Kirschvink, The Upper Olduvai Geomagnetic Field Reversal from Death Valley, California:

A Fold Test of Transitional Directions, Earth and Planetary Science Letters no. 133, (1995), 475-491.
4. John D. Morris, *The Young Earth* (Green Forest, Arkansas: Master Books, 1999), 80.
5. Ibid., 81.
6. "Noah's Ark—Where Did the Water Come From," http://www.christiananswers.net/q-aig/aig-c010.html
7. C. Berlitz, *The Lost Ship of Noah* (London, England: W.H. Allen, 1987), 126.
8. *The Larousse Encyclopedia of Mythology* (London, England: Chancellor Press, 1996), 275-277.
9. Larry Vardiman, *Sea-Floor Sediment and the Age of the Earth* (El Cajon, California: Institute for Creation Research, 1996), 12.

Chapter 10

1. "The Grand Canyon," www.webmecca.com/creation/articles/article36.htm
2. "Halite the Mineral," www.desert.usa.com/mag99/jan/papr/geo_halite.html
3. "The Grand Canyon"
4. Ibid.
5. Michael J. Oard, *An Ice Age Caused by the Genesis Flood* (El Cajon, California: Institute for Creation Research, 1990), 78.
6. Ibid., 78.
7. Larry Vardiman, *Ice Cores and the Age of the Earth* (El Cajon, California: Institute for Creation Research, 1993), 28.
8. Oard, *An Ice Age Caused*, 78.
9. Robert Bedrosian, "Eastern Asia Minor and the Caucasus

in Ancient Mythologies,"
http://www.virtualscape.com/rbedrosian/mythint.htm
10. Oard, *And Ice Age*, 78.
11. "Grand Canyon Legend," Creation Ex Nihilo, vol. 7, no. 4 (1985), 11.

Chapter 11

1. Michael J. Oard, *An Ice Age Caused by the Genesis Flood* (El Cajon, California: Institute for Creation Research, 1990), 94.
2. Ibid., 80.
3. Ibid., 33.
4. Ibid., 98.
5. Larry Vardiman, Ice Cores and the Age of the Earth (El Cajon, California: Institute for Creation Research, 1993), 51.
6. S.L. Vartanyan, Kh.A.H. Arslanov, T.V. Tertychnaya, and S.B. Chernov, "Radiocarbon Dating Evidence for Mammoths on Wrangel Island, Arctic Ocean, Until 2000 B.C.," Journal of Paleontology, vol. 61, no. 6 (1986-87), 198-200.
7. Oard, *An Ice Age Caused*, 117.
8. "Strange Artifacts, Piri Reis Map," http://www.world-mysteries.com/sar_1.htm
9. Ibid
10. John of Fordun, *The Scottichronicon (Chronicle of the Scottish Nation)*, Chapter XII, http://members.aol.com/lochlan2/fordun.htm
11. Bill Cooper, *After The Flood* (West Sussex, England: New Wind Press, 1995), 251.
12. *The Venidad*, Chapter Three: Onslaught of the Evil One,

http://members.ozemail.com.au/~zarathus/chaptr3.html

13. Henry M. Morris, *The Remarkable Record of Job* (Grand Rapids, Michigan: Baker Books, 1996), 29-30.
14. Oard, *An Ice Age Caused,* 84.
15. Dan Vergano, "Sunken Cities Surface in Time," USA Today, 27 June 2001 (World Section), http://usatoday.com/news/world/june01/2001-06-28-sunken-cities.htm
16. Oard, *An Ice Age Caused,* 86.
17. Strange Artifacts.
18. Oard, An Ice Age Caused, 117.

Chapetr 12

1. Michael J. Oard, *An Ice Age Caused by the Genesis Flood* (El Cajon, California: Institute for Creation Research, 1990), 87.
2. G. Haynes, *Mammoths, Mastadonts and Elephants: Biology, Behavior and the Fossil Record* (Cambridge, England: Cambridge University Press, 1991), 48.
3. Oard, *An Ice Age Caused,* 87.
4. Ibid., 88.
5. "Scientists Speak About Radiocarbon Dating," http://www.pathlights.com/ce_encyclopedia/06dat5.htm
6. John D. Morris, *The Young Earth* (Green Forest, Arkansas: Master Books, 1999), 65.
7. Henry M. Morris, *Scientific Creationism* (Green Forest, Arkansas: Master Books, 1998), 161.
8. Morris, *The Young Earth*, 64,82.
9. Ibid., 82.
10. Science, 29 June 2001, 2443-2444, 2453-2458.
11. Jonathan Safarti, "Mammoth, Riddle of the Ice Age,"

Creation Ex Nihilo, vol. 22, no.2 (2000), 14-15.

Chapter 13

1. Marvin L. Lubenow, *Bones of Contention* (Grand Rapids, Michigan: Baker Books, 1994), 39.
2. David T. Moore, *Five Lies of the Century* (Wheaton, Illinois: Tyndale House, 1995), 139.
3. "Lucy Was a Knuckle-Walker," Creation Ex Nihilo, vol. 22, no. 3, (2000), 7.
4. Moore, *Five Lies*, 138.
5. Ibid., 137.
6. Jack Cuozzo, *Buried Alive* (Green Forest, Arkansas: Master Books, 1999), Chapter 27.
7. *The Works of Josephus*, translated by William Whiston (Peabody, Maryland: Hendrickson Publishers, 1996), 35.

Chapter 14

1. Ken Ham, Carl Wieland, and Don Batten, *One Blood* (Green Forest, Arkansas: Master Books, 2001), Chapter 10.
2. Ibid., Chapter 9.
3. "Focus Articles," Creation Ex Nihilo, vol. 18, no. 2, (1995-1996), 7-9.
4. Jack Cuozzo, *Buried Alive* (Green Forest, Arkansas: Master Books, 1999), 251.
5. David T. Moore, *Five Lies of the Century* (Wheaton, Illinois: Tyndale House, 1995), 105.
6. Ham, Wieland, and Batten, *One Blood*, Chapter 2.
7. Ibid., 67.

8. Creation Ex Nihilo Technical Journal, vol. 9, no. 2 (1995), 139-140.
9. Ibid.
10. Don Batten, "Ligers and Wolphins" What Next?, Creation Ex Nihilo, vol. 22, no. 3 (2000), 29.
11. Ibid., 31.
12. Ham, Wieland, and Batten, *One Blood*, 54.

Chapter 15

1. John Woodmorappe, Noah's Ark: A Feasibility Study (El Cajon, California: Institute for Creation Research, 1996), 10.
2. Ibid., Chapter 3.
3. Larry Pierce, "The Largest Ships of Antiquity," Creation Ex Nihilo, vol. 22, no. 3 (2000), 46.
4. Woodmorappe, *Noah's Ark*, 49-50.
5. "Wood," The Oxford Encyclopedia of Archaeology in the Near East, Eric M. Meyers, ed., (New York, New York: Oxford, University Press, 1997), 347-349.
6. "The Working Celtic Cross," E. M. Crichton, http://www.world-mysteries.com/sar_5.htm
7. The Works of Josephus, translated by William Whiston (Peabody, Maryland: Hendrickson Publishers, 1996), 34.
8. "Measuring Noah's Ark," http://brians_annex_ii.tripod.com/noahsarkmeasured.html

Chapter 16

1. Marvin L. Lubenow, *Bones of Contention* (Grand Rapids, Michigan: Baker Books, 1994), Chapter 12.

2. Henry M. Morris, *Scientific Creationism* (Green Forest, Arkansas: Master Books, 1998), 175.
3. Michael J. Oard, And Ice Age Caused by the Genesis Flood (El Cajon, California: Institute for Creation Research, 1990), 94.
4. Duane T. Gish, Dinosaurs by Design (Green Forest, Arkansas: Master Books, 1996), 75.
5. Robert Bedrosian, "Eastern Asia Minor and the Caucasus in Ancient Mythologies," http://rbedrosian.com/mythint.htm
6. N. G. L. Hammond, *A History of Greece* (Oxford, England: Clarendon Press, 1967), 87.

Chapter 17

1. Russell Humphreys, *Starlight and Time* (Green Forest, Arkansas: Master Books, 2002).
2. Russell Humphreys, "A Young Earth Relativistic Cosmology," http://www.pages.org/bcs/bcs051.html
3. Humphreys, *Starlight*, 73.
4. Jonathan Safarti, "Exploding Stars Point to a Young Universe," Creation Ex Nihilo, vol. 9, no. 3 (1997), 46-48.
5. Danny Faulkner, "Comets and the Age of the Solar System," Creation Ex Nihilo Technical Journal, vol. 11, no. 3 (1997), 264-273.

Chapetr 18

1. Tom Van Flandern, Dark Matter Missing Planets and New Comets (Berkley, California: North Atlantic Books,

1993), 235.

2. "The Mazzaroth or Zodiac," http://www.tckillian.com/greg/mazzaroth.html
3. Enuma Elish, The Babylonian Creation Epic, Tablet IV, http://www.piney.com/Enuma4.html
4. Van Flandern, *Dark Matter*, 161.
5. Ibid., 222-225.
6. D. S. Allan and J. B. Delair, "When the Earth Nearly Died," http://dialspace.dial.pipex.com/town/parade/henryr/scispi/atlantic/.htm

Chapter 19

1. John D. Morris, *The Young Earth* (Green Forest, Arkansas: Master Books, 1999), 87.
2. Henry M. Morris, *Scientific Creationism* (Green Forest, Arkansas: Master Books, 1998), 154.
3. Morris, *The Young Earth*, 83.
4. Ibid., 75.
5. Andrew Snelling, "Coal Beds and Noah's Flood," Creation Ex Nihilo, vol. 8, no. 3, 20-21. http://www.answersingenesis.org/docs/1137.asp
6. Ibid.
7. Dave Phillips, "Neanderthals Are Still Human," Impact article no. 323, (Institute for Creation Research, El Cajon, California), http://www.icr.org/pubs/imp/imp-323.htm
8. The Sydney Morning Herald, Sydney, Australia, 21 Feb. 1996, p. 9.
9. Morris, *Scientific Creationism*, 175.

Chapter 20

1. James H. Breasted, *A History of Egypt*, 2nd edition, 23.
2. Sir Alan Gardner, *Egypt of the Pharaohs* (New York, New York: Oxford University Press, 1961), 53.
3. P. John Crowe, "The Revision of Ancient History-A Perspective," section 2.4., http://www.knowledge.co.uk/sis/ancient.htm
4. Ibid.
5. Robert Schoch, "Re-dating the Great Sphinx," http://www.antiquityofman.com/Schock_redating.html
6. Duane T. Gish, *Dinosaurs by Design* (Green Forest, Arkansas: Master Books, 1996), 74.
7. "Ancient Eclipses,"The History Net, http://ancienthistory.about.com/library/weekly/aa080399.htm
8. William Loftus, *Travels and Researches in Chaldea and Sinai* (London, England: James Nisbet, 1857), 29.
9. "The Confusion of the Languages," http://www.varchive.org/itb/confus.htm
10. Larry Pierce, "In the Days of Peleg," Creation Ex Nihilo, vol. 22, no. 1 (2000), 46.
11. Ibid., 47.
12. Ibid.
13. Bill Cooper, *After The Flood* (West Sussex, England: New Wine Press, 1995), 81.
14. Ibid., 104.
15. Ibid., 84.
16. Ibid., 94-95.
17. Ibid., 84.
18. Ibid., 105.
19. Ibid., 46-55.
20. Ibid., 244.

21. *The Works of Josephus*, translated William Whiston (Peabody, Maryland: Hendrickson Publishers, 1996), 35.

Chapter 21

1. Marvin Lubenow, *Bones of Contention* (Grand Rapids, Michigan: Baker Books, 1994), 220.
2. Ibid., 214.
3. Ibid., 217.
4. Ibid., 216.
5. Ibid., 221.
6. *The Works of Josephus*, translated by William Whiston (Peabody, Maryland: Hendrickson Publishers, 1996), 35.
7. Grant Jeffrey, *The Signature of God* (Nashville, Tennessee: Word Publishing, 1998), 40.
8. "The Exodus," http://www.countrylife.org/hero.htm
9. Jeffrey, *The Signature of God*, 39.
10. Rabbi Yakov Kleiman, "The Cohanim/DNA Connection," http://www.aish.com/societywork/sciencenature/The_Cohanim_-_DNA_Connection.asp
11. Jeffrey, *The Signature of God*, 34.
12. *The Works of Josephus*, 38.
13. Randall Price, The Stones Cry Out (Eugene, Oregon: Harvest House Publishers, 1997), 98.
14. Ibid., Chapter 8.
15. Ibid., Chapter 6.
16. Ibid., 82.

Chapter 22

1. C. H. Kang and Ethel R. Nelson, *The Discovery of Genesis*

(St. Louis, Missouri: Concordia Publishing House, 1979), 95.
2. Ibid., 98.
3. Ibid., 98.
4. Ethel R. Nelson, Richard E. Broadberry, and Ginger Tong Chock, *God's Promise to the Chinese* (Dunlap, Tennessee: Read Books Publisher, 1997), 18.
5. Ibid., 27.
6. Ibid., 21.
7. Ibid., 109.
8. Ibid., 30.
9. Ibid., 58.
10. Ibid., 61.
11. Ibid., 99.
12. Ibid., 69.
13. Ibid.
14. Ibid., 9.
15. Ibid., 65.
16. Don Richardson, *Eternity In Their Hearts* (Ventura, California: Regal Books, 1984), 128.
17. Nelson, Broadberry, and Chock, *God's Promise*, 60.
18. Ibid., 51.
19. Ibid., 8.
20. Ibid., 8.
21. Richardson, *Eternity*, 67.

Chapter 23

1. Grant R. Jeffrey, *The Signature of God* (Nashville, Tennessee: Word Publishing, 1998), 209-228.
2. Randall Price, *Secrets of the Dead Sea Scrolls* (Eugene, Oregon: Harvest House, 1996), 76.

3. Ibid., 80.

Chapter 24

1. Matthew 28: 4.
2. James Orr, The Resurrection of Jesus (London, England: Hodder and Stoughton, 1909), 160.
3. Grant Jeffrey, *The Signature of God* (Nashville, Tennessee: Word Publishing, 1998), 336-339.
4. Ibid., 99-100.
5. Ibid., 110.
6. Luke 23: 44-45.
7. Josh McDowell, *Evidence That Demands a Verdict* (Nashville, Tennessee: Thomas Nelson, 1979), 86.
8. Acts 21:20.
9. "Historical Sources on Jesus," http://www.btinternet.com/~nbch/sources.html
10. Ibid.
11. Randall Price, *The Stones Cry Out* (Eugene, Oregon: Harvest House, 1997), 85.

Chapter 25

1. Matthew 1:24.
2. Lambert Dolphin, "The Destruction of the Second Temple," http://www.ldolphin.org/destruct2.html
3. Luke 13:33.
4. Isaiah 11:11-12.
5. Genesis 10:14.
6. Randall Price, *The Stones Cry Out* (Eugene, Oregon: Harvest House, 1997), 222-227.

7. *The Works of Josephus*, edited by William Whitson (Peabody, Maryland: Hendrickson Publishers, 1996), 36.
8. Ibid., 35.
9. Isaiah 11:11-12.
10. Mathew 24:14.
11. II Peter 3:8.
12. Isaiah 2:4.
13. Revelation 20:6.
14. Revelation 13:5-7.
15. Revelation 21:1-2.
16. Romans 11:7-8.

Where Credit Is Due

My earth science training at Dartmouth College in the mid 70's was thorough and informative; however, the information gleaned was presented within an old-earth worldview (faith).

About 1985, I discovered Dr. Henry M. Morris' monumental work, *The Genesis Flood*, which opened my eyes to the reconcilable "discrepancies" that are alleged between Biblical history and "good science." The evidences of the geological processes that I had learned about now logically fit together!

Dr. Morris founded the Institute for Creation Research in El Cajon, California, and has provided fantastic scientific analysis of our world for many years. I am also greatly indebted to Ken Ham and Answers In Genesis, based in Florence, Kentucky. These institutions are superior sources of intellectual honesty in the sciences and theology.

And last, but certainly not least, I thank my mom and dad, Evelyn (Rayzor) and Dr. Les Nienhuis. They have loved me through everything, and encouraged me during my endeavors.

www.GenesisVeracity.com

1-866-GEOFACT